THE ULTIMATE GUIDE TO

TO

COOKING CHICKEN

THE INDIAN WAY

Prasenjeet Kumar

Disclaimers

Although the Author has made every effort to ensure that the information in this book was correct at the time of publication, the Author does not assume and hereby disclaims any liability to any party for any loss, damage, or disruption caused by errors or omissions, whether such errors or omissions result from negligence, accident, or any other cause.

This book is not intended as a substitute for the medical advice of physicians. The reader should regularly consult a physician in matters relating to his/her health and particularly with respect to any symptoms that may require diagnosis or medical attention.

This book also assumes that the reader does not suffer from any food allergies or related medical conditions. Readers suffering from food allergies are requested to skip the recipes that contains ingredients which trigger adverse reactions in that reader or in his/her family and friends.

The spellings used in this book are British, which may look strange to my American friends, but NOT to those living in Australia, Canada, India, Ireland and, of course, the United Kingdom. This means that color is written as colour and so on. I hope that is NOT too confusing!

Table of Contents

I

Chicken—Why Bother?

"There are two types of vegetarians: (1) those who have beef with chicken; and (2) those who are too chicken to have beef."

— **Mokokoma Mokhonoana**

Ah, the conceited, supercilious joys of having red meat!

So does 'bird flu' really scare you more than 'swine flu' or the 'mad cow disease'?

Do you wonder if some people in the world could, in their right senses, instead of plumping for the robust chewiness of the beef, pork, mutton, veal or venison, prefer the "insipid", "characterless" taste of the chicken?

Do you prefer to "beef up" than "chicken out"?

Okay, the last one was unnecessary for this debate.

But the short point is that if you do prefer red meat over white for whatever reason, relax, you are certainly not alone.

But beware; you may be in danger of belonging to a near extinct tribe of people who don't realise the enormous benefits of including the white meat of chicken (or fish) in their daily diets.

Red Meat vs. White Meat Debate

As new scientific research reinforces, chicken has acquired a formidable reputation for being a source of low calorie, high protein, and waist-slimming food that is bristling with zinc, calcium, iron, magnesium and a host of vitamins. To some extent, you can get most of these nutrients also from your favourite prime cut of red meat, but only with some oodles of heart-unhealthy cholesterol that you can't do anything about.

For example, a 3-oz. serving of beef provides 2.9 g of saturated fat, while a similar serving of chicken provides only 0.9 mg of saturated fat. Similarly, chicken is a more appropriate choice for calorie-conscious people because a serving of chicken provides 142 calories, whereas a serving of beef provides 173 calories.

Otherwise, according to the USDA , chicken (100 g) has energy (215 kcal), protein (18 g), fat (15 g), saturated fat (4 g), cholesterol (75 mg), Calcium (11 mg), Iron (0.9 mg), Magnesium (20 mg), Phosphorous (147 mg), Potassium (189 mg), Sodium (70 mg), and Zinc (1.3 mg). It also contains Vitamin C, Thiamin, Riboflavin, Niacin, Vitamin B-6, Folate, Vitamin B-12, Vitamin A, Vitamin E, Vitamin D, and Vitamin K.

The Ubiquitous Chicken

To be sure, you can't avoid chicken wherever you go, because it is the most common type of poultry in the world. Chicken has been domesticated and consumed as food for thousands of years.

Indians believe that chickens were first domesticated in India primarily for cockfighting, and only much later for meat. India's jungles are still full of the wild chicken which the world knows as the Red Malay Game Fowl. Another breed called the Black Cochin, as the name suggests, originated from the Cochin area of South India.

Later, chickens spread to other parts of Asia, Africa, and Europe. In the Americas, they were obviously brought from Europe by the early immigrants and colonists.

In the later part of 19th and the early 20th century, chicken rearing on an industrial scale emerged as a big business due to the demand from increasing populations. This large-scale chicken "farming" gave rise to many "industrial" breeds, the two most famous being the Rhode Island Red and the White Leghorn.

Health Benefits of Chicken

Researchers by now have been able to catalogue as many as a dozen solid reasons for adding a portion of chicken to your diet to improve your overall health. These are:

Building Muscles: With 18 g of protein per 100 g, Chicken is a wonderful protein supplier to people's diets. The recommended amount of daily protein requirements for an average person is 1 gram per 1 kg of body weight, or 0.4 g of protein per pound of body weight. So a 200g serving of Chicken can alone meet the 50% daily requirement of protein for a 72 Kg. healthy person.

Heart Healthy: Chicken has Niacin which helps lower cholesterol. Chicken also cuts the risk of heart attacks because it is rich in Vitamin B 6 which helps lower the levels of homocysteine that can cause cardiac arrests. Both help control the blood pressure as well. The American Heart Association has, therefore, advised consuming chicken (or fish) instead of red meat for a lowered risk of heart disease development.

Improves Immunity: From time immemorial, it has been believed that taking warm chicken soup provides relief from common cold, and its closely associated symptoms of a congested nose and a sore throat. This is because chicken has lots of trace minerals that boost the immune system. Specifically, chicken has Zinc which helps to maintain a healthy appetite. No doubt, some clever writers now provide "Chicken Soup for the Soul" as well!

Keeps bones healthy: Chicken has Phosphorus and Calcium, which together keep your bones healthy. So it helps growing children as well as women who may be prone to osteoporosis.

Relieves Stress: The Vitamin B 5 or Pantothenic Acid, which chicken has, is believed to have a calming effect on the nerves. Another amino acid called Tryptophan gives you that comforting feeling that you get after consuming a big bowl of your grandma's chicken soup. In fact, if you're feeling depressed, eating some chicken is almost guaranteed to increase your Serotonin levels, enhance your mood, blast stress, and even lull you to sleep.

Soothes PMS Symptoms: The Magnesium in chicken is known to help women cope with pre-menstrual stress.

Spikes Testosterone Levels: For men, the Zinc in chicken helps to regulate the testosterone (male hormone) levels.

Weight Loss: Diets with high levels of protein (e.g. the Atkins Diet) have been known to be effective in reducing weight. Chicken has been a good candidate for inclusion in such diets, along with lentils and nuts, as they all provide high protein levels without too much of saturated fat.

Cuts Risk Of Arthritis: Chicken is rich in Selenium which cuts the risk of developing arthritis at later stages of life.

Reduces Cancer Risk: A higher consumption of red meat (e.g. beef, pork, mutton etc) has been held responsible for increasing the risk of colorectal cancer. This risk reduces substantially if a switchover to white meat, such as chicken (or fish), is made.

Convinced somewhat?

Let's then proceed to how you can include chicken in your diet in the most flavourful ways that are known to mankind.

Food for Thought

"The key to everything is patience. You get the chicken by hatching the egg, not by smashing it."

---Arnold H. Glasow

II

Cooking Chicken the Indian Way

"And believe me, a good piece of chicken can make anybody believe in the existence of God."

— Sherman Alexie, The Absolutely True Diary of a Part-Time Indian

With such a robust chicken-cooking tradition in place, it is difficult to believe that the ancient Chinese or Indians once considered the duck to be a cleaner bird than the chicken. This was probably because since the former lives on water, it is presumed to be at least well-washed!

More pertinently, the duck is not seen to be pecking on everything like the chicken does. That's probably why you can have "Peking Duck' but not 'Peking Chicken'.

Anyone interacting with the peripatetic Indian businessmen, who hail predominantly from the western Indian states of Gujarat or Rajasthan, would think that Indians are primarily vegetarians. Once in India, they are then justifiably shocked to find a flourishing omnivorous tradition.

Some attribute this to the influence of the medieval rulers who came from Turkey, Persia or any of the Central Asian States like Uzbekistan. This is evident from the very popular body of dishes that goes around under the banner of Mughlai cuisine.

Certainly much of the baking tradition, especially using tandoors (earthen ovens) would have come from these regions. But barbeque, I'm not so sure that it is not as ancient as the discovery of fire and roasting of the hunt-of-the-day thereon.

Most Asian traditions of cooking chicken employ a number of flavourful techniques to mask whatever little "smell" the raw chicken may have acquired in its journey from the farm or the range to your plate.

This in the Thai tradition could mean the use of Galangal, Kafir Lime leaves and Lemongrass. The Chinese would, of course, be liberal with their Soya Sauce, Chilli Sauce and Fish Oil. The Japanese would often be quite frugal with their spicing but they would compensate that with the most exquisitely carved sushi rolls that your mind can ever conjure.

But the Indians use nothing that the Chinese, Japanese, Thai or the Koreans are so fond of. Instead they seem to dunk their chicken in almost everything that grows in their own backyards and still manage to come up with a mind-boggling number of flavourful preparations.

Indians are also unique in using pressure cookers for cooking chicken. This not only economises on the use of fuel or electricity but also very cleverly destroys bugs, including the one causing bird flu. The Indian preference for using the free-range and freshly slaughtered chicken also helps to contain salmonella contamination to some extent.

This book is a humble attempt to catalogue 51 mouth-watering "Home-Style" ways to cooking chicken in a JIFFY as only Indians Can. You will learn to cook chicken with yoghurt and coconut milk, mustard and turmeric, curry leaves and garam masala (literally hot spices) and so on.

So forget your chicken nuggets, wings, wraps, and sandwiches. Also say bye to the boring boiled and broiled and baked ways to make chicken and egg dishes and let this new book open your eyes to the wonderful possibilities of cooking chicken the way northern, southern, eastern and western Indians do.

There are 7 starter (or snack) dishes, 8 dry recipes, 15 chicken curries, 5 recipes for cooking chicken with rice, and 8 ways to cook eggs the Indian way. For the spice-challenged or nostalgia ridden folks, there are

8 dishes from the days of the British Raj that do use cheese and involve baking, if you were missing that!

And the bottom line is that you master these and you can handle any Indian non-vegetarian dish, I promise.

N.B. Please remember that the "Home Style" recipes that I have catalogued here are made regularly in my home. You are strongly encouraged to experiment, adapt and add your own variation so that the food tastes like your "Home food".

A word of warning though. If you are a complete newbie i.e. someone who does not even know how to boil an egg, then I suggest you start from my first book "How To Cook In A Jiffy Even If You Have Never Boiled An Egg Before" (see the description towards the end of this book).

Indian cooking can be a little tricky and it is best to acquire some basic cooking skills before making this a part of your daily routine.

Chapter 1

Chicken Entrées or Starters

"My favorite dish is tandoori chicken."

--Shah Rukh Khan

You can pardon Shah Rukh Khan for showing preference for a chicken dish from his original home place Peshawar.

But that can't negate the fact that tandoori chicken has become the commonest chicken dish that every dhaba (way side eatery) in Northern India can serve with aplomb.

It is also a great party dish, something that is served with drinks, before the Great Indian Dinner is served.

This chapter focuses on 7 such party dishes that can be ordered as Entrée or Snacks, with drinks, while you wait for your main dish.

"Traditional Tandoori" Chicken

Tandoori chicken, as we just mentioned, is that ubiquitous dish that all restaurants from 5-star to wayside eateries in India serve with equal felicity.

For the really authentic taste, you would need a tandoor, an earthen oven buried in earth, which is not very practical for most homes even in India. So some people use a "gas tandoor" while most others make do with an oven or a grill, to almost achieve the same taste.

We present the 'Grill option' here.

Serves 3-4

Ingredients

Whole Chicken -1 but cut into 8 pieces (or choose your favourite pieces)

Note: If frozen, please thaw the chicken first.

Yoghurt unsweetened-200 grams (7oz) (1 cup) Indian set curd is preferred.

Ginger-2 inches chopped finely

Garlic-6 cloves chopped finely

Tomato sauce/ketchup-2 tablespoon

Garam Masala-1/2 teaspoon

Tip: If you can't get ready-made garam masala mixture from a nearby Indian store, you can make yours by using 1 black cardamom, 3 green cardamoms, 4 cloves, and 1 inch cinnamon-all ground together for this dish.

Kashmiri Red chilli powder (not the hot variety)-1/4 teaspoon

Green Chillies-2 (deseeded and chopped, just for the flavour)

Coriander (Dhania) leaves- a bunch chopped

Salt- 1 teaspoon or to taste

Juice of Lemon-1

Ghee (clarified butter) or butter (or any cooking oil)- 1 tablespoon

Method

In a bowl, beat together all the ingredients and marinate the chicken in this mixture.

Set aside for 4 hours or in the fridge overnight.

Heat the grill and place the chicken pieces on it along with some marinade.

Gently turn over every five minutes till the chicken pieces are cooked to your liking.

Serve with fresh onions and slices of lemon.

That's all. Your "Traditional Tandoori" Chicken is now ready.

Prep time: 10 minutes (excluding marinating time)

Cooking time: 30 minutes

Total time: 40 minutes

Chicken Amritsari

Named after Amritsar, the famous holy town for Sikhs (and Hindus) in Punjab, this is another classic dish from North India that is a favourite party dish as well.

Serves 3-4

Ingredients

Boneless Chicken-1/2 Kg (18oz) (2 cups); cut into bite-size pieces

Note: If frozen, please thaw the chicken first.

Kashmiri Red Chilli powder-1/2 teaspoon (This imparts more colour and flavour and does not make it hot).

Turmeric (Haldi)-1 teaspoon

Garlic paste- 1 teaspoon

Carom seeds (Ajwain) - ½ teaspoon

Asafoetida (Hing) - ½ teaspoon

Coriander (Dhania) seeds (whole) - 1 teaspoon

Chickpea flour (Besan) - ½ cup

Rice flour- 1 tablespoon

Baking powder- ½ teaspoon

Dried Mango (Amchoor) powder- ½ teaspoon OR Lemon juice- 1 tablespoon

Salt- ½ teaspoon or to taste

Water- 1 cup

Yoghurt unsweetened-100 grams (3.5oz) (1/2 cup) Indian set curd is preferred.

Cooking Oil (enough to deep fry) – quantity would depend on the size of your wok/deep frying pan

Method

Except the chicken and the oil, mix all other ingredients in a bowl.

Add the water and beat until smooth and light.

The batter should be of a thin coating consistency.

Add the chicken and set it aside for at least one hour. This helps the besan (chickpea flour) to absorb the water well and attain a thicker consistency. Also the chicken will be marinated and will cook better.

If the batter becomes too thick, you may add a little more water and beat well.

Heat oil in a frying pan or wok.

Take the chicken, a tablespoonful at a time, along with the mixture, and drop into the hot oil.

Be careful of the splatter that follows.

You will find that the mixture swells up.

Gently turn them around and take out from the oil when they are nice and golden brown.

Remove to a dish which is covered with a paper napkin so that all the excess oil can be absorbed.

Repeat till all the chicken pieces are fried.

That's all. Your Chicken Amritsari is ready to be served.

Enjoy with any of the chutneys, especially the mint chutney.

Prep time: 15 minutes (excluding marinating time)

Cooking time: 15 minutes

Total time: Approximately 30 minutes

Chicken Pakoras (Fritters)

If you prefer a less spicy version of the Amritsari Chicken, you can give this recipe from Eastern India a try. This dish requires NO marination; so can be prepared when you just can't wait.

Serves 3-4

Ingredients

Boneless boiled chicken-1/2 Kg (18oz) (2 cups); cut into bite-size pieces

Chick pea flour (Besan)-1 cup

Rice flour-1/2 cup

Baking powder-1/2 teaspoon

Asafoetida (Hing)-1/2 teaspoon

Coriander (Dhania) powder-1 teaspoon

Cumin seeds (Jeera)-1/2 teaspoon

Turmeric (Haldi)-1/2 teaspoon

Red Chilli powder-1/2 teaspoon

Salt-1/2 teaspoon or to taste

Water-1 cup (approximately)

Cooking Oil (enough to deep fry) – quantity would depend on the size of your wok/deep frying pan

Method

Mix all the ingredients, except the chicken and the oil.

Add the water and beat until smooth and light.

The mixture should be of a thin coating consistency. Set it aside for at least 15 minutes. This helps the flour to absorb the water well and attain a thicker consistency.

If it becomes too thick, you may add a little more water and beat well.

Now add the chicken to the batter.

Heat oil in a frying pan or wok.

Take the mixture with the chicken, a tablespoonful at a time, and drop into the hot oil.

Be careful of the splatter that follows.

You will find that the fritters swell up.

Gently turn them around and take out from the oil when they are nice and golden brown.

Remove to a dish which is covered with a paper napkin so that all the excess oil can be absorbed.

Repeat till all the fritters/pakoras are fried.

That's all. Your crispy Chicken Pakoras are ready.

Enjoy with any of the chutneys.

Prep time: 15 minutes (excluding boiling time for chicken)

Cooking time: 15 minutes

Total time: Approximately 30 minutes

Chicken Malai Tikka (Grilled Boneless Chicken in a Cream Marinade)

Chicken Malai Tikka is again a very popular party/ entrée dish that most restaurants from 5-star to wayside eateries in India can offer without much ado.

We present here a version that can be made without a tandoor on a conventional grill.

Serves 3-4

Ingredients

Boneless Chicken -1/2 Kg (18oz) (2 cups) cut into bite-sized pieces

Yoghurt unsweetened (Indian set curd is preferred)- 200 grams (7oz) (1 cup)

Fresh Cream- 100 grams (1/2 cup)

Ginger-2 inches chopped finely

Garlic-6 cloves chopped finely

Cheddar cheese-2 tablespoon grated

Almonds- 12 pieces ground into a paste

Garam Masala-1/2 teaspoon

Tip: If you can't get ready-made garam masala mixture from a nearby Indian store, you can make yours by using 1 black cardamom, 3 green

cardamoms, 4 cloves, and 1 inch cinnamon-all ground together for this dish.

Kashmiri Red chilli powder (not the hot variety)-1/4 teaspoon

Green Chillies-2 (deseeded and chopped, just for flavour)

Coriander (Dhania) leaves- a bunch chopped

Salt- 1 teaspoon or to taste

Sugar- ½ teaspoon

Lemon Juice -1 teaspoon

Ghee (clarified butter) or butter (or any cooking oil)- 1 tablespoon

Method

In a bowl, beat together all the ingredients and marinate the chicken in this mixture.

Set aside for 4 hours or overnight in the fridge.

Heat the grill and the place the chicken pieces on it along with some marinade.

Gently turn over every five minutes or till the chicken pieces are cooked to your liking.

That's all. Your Chicken Malai Tikka is now ready.

Prep time: 10 minutes (excluding marinating time)

Cooking time: 30 minutes

Total time: 40 minutes

Chicken Chilly Indian Style

Obviously inspired by the Chinese, who are just across the border, this dish from the North-Eastern part of India makes a good party dish, especially among the college going crowd.

Just on this ground, therefore, I overrule the protestations of the purists, and dare to include this dish in the Entrée section here.

Serves 3-4

Ingredients

Chicken boiled -1/2 Kg (18oz) (2 cups) cut into bite-sized pieces

Onion (sliced)-3

Chopped Garlic- 12 cloves (2 tablespoon)

Green Bell Pepper (sliced) - 2

Dark Soya sauce- 2 tablespoon

White Vinegar- 1 tablespoon

Corn Flour- 2 tablespoon (dissolved in a cup of water)

Salt- 1 teaspoon or to taste

Sugar- ½ teaspoon

Cooking Oil -2 tablespoon (Use a milder flavoured oil such as groundnut, sesame, or rice bran for the best effect)

Method

Place a wok on your heat source and pour in the cooking oil.

When the oil heats up, add the chopped garlic and sauté till it gives a nice aroma.

Immediately add the sliced onions and stir well.

Sauté for a few minutes and add the sliced bell peppers.

Now add the Soya sauce and the Vinegar. Mix well.

Add the chicken, salt and the sugar.

Pour the dissolved corn flour over and let this mixture come to a boil.

Reduce heat and cook for 2 minutes or till the sauce is reduced to your taste.

Switch off the heat source.

That's all. Your Chicken Chilly Indian Style is ready.

Prep time: 10 minutes

Cooking time: 10 minutes

Total time: 20 minutes

Roasted Instant "Tandoori" Chicken

Roast chicken is a great favourite of the British, while Tandoori chicken is a ubiquitous dish that all restaurants from 5-star to wayside eateries in India serve with equal felicity. This recipe tries to combine the deliciousness of the roast chicken with the tanginess of the tandoori, without requiring you to invest in a Tandoor (a big earthen oven) or even a grill. You also don't need to marinate the chicken.

Serves 3-4

Ingredients

Whole Chicken -1 but cut into 8 pieces (or choose your favourite pieces)

Yoghurt unsweetened (Indian set curd is preferred)-200 grams (7oz) (1 cup)

Ginger-2 inches chopped finely

Garlic-6 cloves chopped finely

Tomato sauce/ketchup-2 tablespoon

Garam Masala-1/2 teaspoon

Tip: If you can't get ready-made garam masala mixture from a nearby Indian store, you can make yours by using 1 black cardamom, 3 green cardamoms, 4 cloves, and 1 inch cinnamon-all ground together for this dish.

Kashmiri Red Chilli powder (not the hot variety)-1/4 teaspoon

Salt- 1 teaspoon or to taste

Juice of Lemon-1

Ghee (clarified butter) or butter (or any cooking oil)-1 tablespoon

Method using a pressure cooker

In a bowl, beat together all the ingredients EXCEPT the chicken.

In a pressure cooker, add the chicken and the beaten ingredients together (unlike traditional tandoori chicken, you don't need to marinate the chicken with the beaten ingredients first).

Close the lid of the pressure cooker with weight and put it on your heat source.

Let it come to full pressure (i.e. when the weight lifts and there is a whistling sound).

Immediately reduce the heat (to SIM on a gas stove) and let the chicken cook for 5 more minutes before turning off the heat source.

Let the cooker cool down on its own.

In a non-stick pan, add the butter and put it on your heat source.

Let the butter melt.

Slowly add the chicken and the juices from the cooker.

Let all the water evaporate.

Gently turn the chicken to give it a golden brown colour.

That's all. Your instant Roasted "Tandoori" Chicken is now ready.

If using a thick bottomed pan or wok

In a bowl, beat together all the ingredients EXCEPT the chicken.

In a wok/pan, add the chicken and the beaten ingredients together (unlike traditional tandoori chicken, you don't need to marinate the chicken with the beaten ingredients first).

Place the wok/pan on your heat source.

As soon as the mixture comes to a boil, reduce the heat (to SIM on a gas stove), cover with a lid and let the chicken cook for 20 more minutes (or till the chicken is cooked to your liking) before turning off the heat source.

If the mixture becomes too dry while cooking, you may add a little water to prevent the mixture from burning.

In another non-stick pan, add the butter and put it on your heat source.

Let the butter melt.

Slowly add the chicken and the juices from the pan/wok.

Let all the water evaporate.

Gently turn the chicken to give it a golden brown colour.

That's all. Your instant Roasted "Tandoori" Chicken is now ready.

Prep time: 10 minutes

Cooking time: 20 minutes with a pressure cooker; 40-45 minutes with a wok

Total time: 30 minutes with a pressure cooker; 50-55 minutes with a wok

Chapter 2

Latpat (Dry) Chicken Recipes

These are recipes which generally have NO curry. So, these go well with all kinds of breads, including the Indian Naan or Roti. These have a thick sauce, and so are not as "dry" as the entree dishes. For want of a better word, however, we are categorising these exotic recipes under the "dry" category.

For eating with rice, however, Indians do prefer a curry chicken dish, which we shall discuss in the next chapter.

Murg Jhalfrezi (Chicken Fried)

Serves 3-4

Ingredients

Whole Chicken -1 but cut into 8 pieces (or choose your favourite pieces)

Yoghurt unsweetened (Indian set curd is preferred)-200 grams (7oz) (1 cup)

Ginger-2 inches chopped finely

Onions- 2-3 large, thinly sliced

Garlic-6 cloves chopped finely

Garam Masala-1/2 teaspoon

Tip: If you can't get ready-made garam masala mixture from a nearby Indian store, you can make yours by using 1 black cardamom, 3 green cardamoms, 4 cloves, and 1 inch cinnamon-all ground together for this dish.

Kashmiri Red chilli powder (not the hot variety)-1/4 teaspoon

Coriander (Dhania) powder- a teaspoon

Salt- 1 teaspoon or to taste

Ghee (clarified butter) or butter (or any cooking oil)-2 tablespoon

Water- ½ cup

Method

In a bowl, beat together all the ingredients (except the onions and the oil/ghee) and marinate the chicken in the mixture.

Set aside for 4 hours or overnight in the fridge.

Place a wok/deep pan on your heat source and add the oil.

As the oil heats up, add the sliced onions and fry till it turns golden.

Remove from the wok and keep aside.

Take out the chicken pieces from the marinade and put it in the wok/pan.

Fry the chicken pieces till they are brown on all sides.

Now add the marinade and let the chicken simmer for about 10 minutes or till it is cooked to your liking.

Stir in the fried onions and simmer for 2 more minutes.

That's all. Your Murg Jhalfrezi or Chicken Fried Indian Style is now ready.

Prep time: 10 minutes (excluding marinating time)

Cooking time: 20 minutes

Total time: 30 minutes

Chicken Do Pyaza (Chicken with Fried Onions)

Again a popular North Indian dish that goes well with Rotis, the Indian unleavened bread.

Serves 3-4

Ingredients

Chicken boneless boiled--1/2 kg (18oz) (2 cups)

Onion-1 large (chopped)

Ginger-2 inch piece

Garlic-8 Cloves

Tomatoes-3 (chopped)

(Onion + Ginger + Garlic + Tomatoes blended and made into a fine paste)

Onion- 2 large (chopped) separately for frying

Garam Masala-1/2 teaspoon

Tip: If you can't get ready-made garam masala mixture from a nearby Indian store, you can make yours by using 1 black cardamom, 3 green cardamoms, 4 cloves, and 1 inch cinnamon-all ground together for this dish.

Salt--1 teaspoon (or to taste)

Turmeric (Haldi)--1 and 1/2 teaspoon (1 teaspoon for marinating the chicken and half for the curry.)

Red Chilli powder-- 1/4 teaspoon (enough only to add flavour and not to make it spicy.)

Fresh green chillies whole--4 (Whole chillies impart a lovely flavour to the cuisine and will NOT make it spicy.)

Mustard oil--3 tablespoon (If you want that classic taste, otherwise whatever oil you normally use.)

Water-1/2 cup (roughly 125 ml)

(You may prefer to use the water that was used for boiling the chicken for added taste.)

Vessels: One non-stick frying pan and one kadai (wok)

Method

In a wok, add the oil and put the wok on your heat source.

As the oil heats up, add the chopped onions and fry till they turn golden.

Remove from the wok and keep aside.

Now put the onion+ garlic + ginger+ tomato paste in the wok and stir well.

Add the salt, garam masala, turmeric and red chilli powder.

Keep on stirring till the paste is fried and you can see the oil glistening on the sides of the wok.

Now add the boiled chicken and stir well.

Add ½ cup of water and let the water come to a boil.

Now add the whole fresh green chillies and the fried onions.

Reduce the heat to the minimum (SIM on a gas stove) and cook it for 5 more minutes.

That's all. Your Chicken Do Pyaza (Chicken with fried onions) is ready.

Prep time: 10 minutes (excluding the chicken boiling time)

Cooking time: 15 minutes

Total time: 25 minutes

Chicken 'Ishtew' Mughlai

A take on the British Chicken Stew that is served even today by legendary restaurants like Karim's in the streets around the Red Fort in old Delhi.

Serves 3-4

Ingredients

Chicken pieces-1 Kg (2 lbs) (4 cups)

Onions chopped finely-1 Kg (2 lbs) (4 cups)

Tomatoes chopped-1 Kg (2 lbs) (4 cups)

Garlic chopped-8 cloves

Ginger chopped-2 inch piece

Green Cardamom (Chhoti Elaichi)-4

Brown Cardamom (Badi Elaichi)-2

Cinnamon (Dalchinni)-1 inch stick

Cloves (Laung)-6

Bay Leaves (Tejpatta)-2

Cumin Seeds (Jeera)-1 teaspoon

Yoghurt unsweetened (Indian set curd is preferred)-200 grams (7oz) (1 cup)

Cooking Oil-4 tablespoon

Salt- 1 teaspoon or to taste

Method

Marinate the chicken pieces with yoghurt and salt for half an hour.

Method using pressure cooker

Light the heat source and place the pressure cooker on it. Add the cooking oil.

As soon as the oil warms up, add the cardamom, bay leaves, cinnamon, cloves and the cumin seeds. Let them brown for a few seconds.

Add the garlic and ginger and again let the mixture roast for a minute.

Add the chicken along with the marinade and stir well.

Cover the chicken first with the onions and then with the tomatoes. DO NOT STIR. This is because the chicken has to cook in the juice of the onions and the tomatoes and if we stir at this moment then the onions and tomatoes will get fried (a result that we don't want).

Close the lid of the cooker and let it come to full pressure (i.e. when the weight lifts and there is a whistling sound).

Immediately reduce the heat (to SIM on a gas stove) and let the chicken cook for 5 more minutes before turning off the heat source.

Let the cooker cool down before you open it. You will find that there is a lot of water inside. So light the heat source again and place the cooker on it.

Let the water evaporate till it becomes a thickish curry.

That's all. Your Chicken 'Ishtew' Mughlai is ready.

Using a wok or thick bottomed pan

Switch on your heat source and place the wok/pan on it.

Add the cooking oil.

As soon as the oil warms up, add the cardamom, bay leaves, cinnamon, cloves and the cumin seeds (jeera). Let them brown for a few seconds.

Add the garlic and ginger and again let it roast for a minute.

Add the chicken along with the marinade and stir well.

Cover it with the onions and then with the tomatoes. DO NOT STIR.

This is because the chicken has to cook in the juice of the onions and the tomatoes and if we stir at this moment then the onions and tomatoes will get fried (a result that we don't want).

Cover the wok/pan with a lid and let this all cook till the chicken is well done (in about 20 minutes).

If after 20 minutes, you find that there is some water inside, continue cooking till all that water evaporates and you get a somewhat thickish curry.

That's all. Your Chicken 'Ishtew' Mughlai is ready.

Prep time: 10 minutes (excluding marination time)

Cooking time: 20 minutes with a pressure cooker; 40 minutes with a wok/pan

Total time: 30 minutes with a pressure cooker; 50 minutes with a wok/pan

Murg Mussalam (Chicken stuffed with Mince)

This is a great Mughlai dish that you should attempt only when you want to "shock and awe" your guests. Purists would insist that you use a full chicken for this recipe but if you find that difficult to handle you can always use your favourite "cut" pieces, without compromising on the taste.

Serves 3-4

Ingredients for the filling

Chicken mince--250 grams or 9oz or 1 cup

Medium size Onions--1 (chopped)

Garlic-4 pieces (chopped)

Ginger-1 inch (chopped)

Tomato puree- 3 tablespoon

Turmeric powder (Haldi) - 1/2 tea spoon

Garam Masala (mixture of common Indian spices) crushed- 1/2   tea spoon

Tip: If you can't get ready-made garam masala mixture from a nearby Indian store, you can make yours by using 1 black cardamom, 3 green cardamoms, 4 cloves, and 1 inch cinnamon-all ground together for this dish.

Kashmiri Red Chilli powder--1/4 tea spoon (Recommended for colour, but if you like your dish to be really spicy, use any other red chilli powder)

Cumin whole (Jeera)-1/2 tea spoon

Salt-1/2 tea spoon (or to taste)

Sugar- ½ teaspoon

Cooking oil-1 table spoon

Ghee (clarified butter)-1 tea spoon

Method using a wok/pan

Blend together (in a blender preferably!) the onions, garlic, and ginger to a fine paste.

Heat the oil in a wok/pan.

Add cumin seeds to the oil and as they turn brown, add this paste and gently fry.

As the paste starts giving off a nice aroma, add the chicken mince to it and sauté lightly.

Add the turmeric, red chilli powder, garam masala, salt, sugar and tomato puree to this mixture and keep stirring on a low flame (SIM on a gas stove) till it starts becoming dry.

At this juncture, add the Ghee for a lovely taste.

Stir well and switch off your heat source.

Ingredients for the Chicken

Whole Chicken -1 (uncut) weighing around 1 Kg (2 lbs)

Yoghurt unsweetened (Indian set curd is preferred)-200 grams (7oz) (1 cup)

Ginger-2 inches chopped finely

Garlic-6 cloves chopped finely

Garam Masala-1/2 teaspoon

Tip: If you can't get ready-made garam masala mixture from a nearby Indian store, you can make yours by using 1 black cardamom, 3 green cardamoms, 4 cloves, and 1 inch cinnamon-all ground together for this dish.

Kashmiri Red Chilli powder (not the hot variety)-1/4 teaspoon

Salt- 1 teaspoon or to taste

Sugar- ½ teaspoon

Ghee (clarified butter) or butter (or any oil)-2 tablespoon

Method

In a bowl, beat together all the ingredients (except the oil/ghee) and marinate the chicken in the mixture.

Set aside for 4 hours or overnight in the fridge.

Then take the chicken out and stuff the chicken mince filling that you just made.

Truss the chicken, using a sewing thread, tying legs together and tucking the wings underneath.

Place a wok/deep pan on your heat source and add the oil.

As the oil heats up, add the whole chicken stuffed with chicken mince and gently turn till brown on all sides.

Now add the marinade and let the chicken simmer for about 10 minutes or till it is cooked to your liking.

Keep stirring till all the water evaporates.

That's all. Your Murg Mussalam (Chicken stuffed with mince) is now ready.

Prep time: 20 minutes (excluding marinating time)

Cooking time: 30 minutes

Total time: 50 minutes

Chicken Tikkas (Boneless Barbequed Chicken)

Another classic entrée or party dish, which appeals to people of all ages.

Serves 3-4

Ingredients

Boneless Chicken -1/2 Kg (18oz) (2 cups) cut into bite-sized pieces

Note: If frozen, please thaw the chicken first.

Yoghurt unsweetened (Indian set curd is preferred)-100 grams (4oz) (1/2 cup)

Ginger-2 inches chopped finely

Garlic-6 cloves chopped finely

Tomato sauce/ketchup-2 tablespoon

Garam Masala-1/2 teaspoon

Tip: If you can't get ready-made garam masala mixture from a nearby Indian store, you can make yours by using 1 black cardamom, 3 green cardamoms, 4 cloves, and 1 inch cinnamon-all ground together for this dish.

Kashmiri Red Chilli powder (not the hot variety)-1/4 teaspoon

Green Chillies-2 (deseeded and chopped, just for flavour)

Coriander (Dhania) leaves- a bunch chopped

Salt- 1 teaspoon or to taste

Juice of Lemon-1

Ghee (clarified butter) or butter (or any oil)-1 tablespoon

Onions sliced- 2

Green Capsicum sliced- 1

Method

In a bowl, beat together all the ingredients, except the oil, onion and the green capsicum, and marinate the chicken in the mixture.

Set aside for 4 hours or in the fridge overnight.

Heat the grill and place the chicken pieces, preferably threaded on a skewer, on it without the marinade.

Gently turn over every five minutes till the chicken is cooked to your liking.

Keep aside.

In a wok/pan, heat the oil/ghee and add the sliced onion.

Stir till the onions become translucent.

Now add the green capsicum and the grilled chicken along with all the marinade.

Stir till the chicken is fairly dry.

That's all. Your Chicken Tikka is ready.

Enjoy with your favourite drink.

Prep time: 10 minutes (excluding marinating time)

Cooking time: 30 minutes

Total time: 40 minutes

Chicken 65

This is the fiery chicken fry variation from the South Indian state of Andhra Pradesh. Fortunately, this recipe despite the name doesn't need 65 ingredients!

Serves 3-4

Ingredients

Boneless chicken-1/2 Kg (18oz) (2 cups); cut into bite-size pieces

Note: If frozen, please thaw the chicken first.

For the marinade:

Corn flour- 2 tablespoon

Baking powder-1/2 teaspoon

Coriander powder-1 teaspoon

Cumin seeds (Jeera)-1/2 teaspoon

Black pepper (crushed) - ¼ teaspoon

Turmeric (Haldi)-1/2 teaspoon

Red Chilli powder-1/2 teaspoon

Ginger paste-1/2 teaspoon

Garlic paste-1/2 teaspoon

Lemon juice- 1 tablespoon

Egg- 1 (lightly beaten)

Salt-1/2 teaspoon or to taste

For the spice mixture

Cooking oil- 1 tablespoon

Chopped Garlic- 1 teaspoon

Chopped Ginger- 1 teaspoon

Curry leaves- 20 approx.

Green Chillies (deseeded) - 3

Yoghurt unsweetened (Indian set curd is preferred)-
50 grams (1/4 cup)

Black Pepper (crushed) - ¼ teaspoon

Red Chilli paste- ½ teaspoon

Tomato ketchup- 1 tablespoon

Salt- 1/2 teaspoon or to taste

AND

Cooking Oil (enough to deep fry) – quantity depends
on the size of your wok/deep frying pan

Method

Mix all the ingredients for the marinade and add the
chicken pieces.

Set aside for one hour.

Heat oil in a frying pan or wok.

Take the mixture with the chicken, a tablespoonful at a time, and drop into the hot oil.

Be careful of the splatter that follows.

Gently turn them around and take out from the oil when they are nice and golden brown.

Repeat till all the chicken is fried. Keep aside

Put a pan on your heat source and add one tablespoon of oil. You can use the oil which you have used for frying the chicken.

When the oil heats up, add the curry leaves and the green chillies.

As soon as these start spluttering, add the chopped garlic and ginger. Sauté for a minute till it starts giving off a nice aroma.

Please make sure that your spices don't burn.

Add the remaining ingredients and stir well.

Now add the fried chicken to this spicy mixture and toss till all the chicken is coated well.

That's all. Your Chicken 65 is ready.

Prep time: 15 minutes (excluding marinating time)

Cooking time: 20 minutes

Total time: Approximately 35 minutes (excluding marinating time)

Chicken Shami Kebab

Traditionally made with mutton mince, this is another wonderful dish that can also be served as entrée. The use of lentils improves the nutritional quotient of this dish by many notches.

Serves 3-4

Ingredients

Chicken mince-2 cup (500 grams)

Chana Dal (Split Chick Pea) -1/2 cup (125 grams); soaked in water for at least 4 hours

Chopped Garlic-4 cloves

Chopped Ginger-1 inch

Garam Masala (mixture of common Indian spices)-1/2 teaspoon

Tip: If you can't get ready-made garam masala mixture from a nearby Indian store, you can make yours by using 1 black cardamom, 3 green cardamoms, 4 cloves, and 1 inch cinnamon-all ground together for this dish.

Red Chilli Powder-1/4 teaspoon

Egg- 1 (slightly beaten)

Salt- 1 teaspoon or to taste

Sugar- ¼ teaspoon

Cooking Oil-2 tablespoon

Optional: Fresh Coriander (Cilantro) leaves- 2 tablespoon (chopped)

Green Chilli- 1 (deseeded and chopped)

Method

In a wok/pan, add ½ tablespoon cooking oil and put it on your heat source.

As soon as the oil heats up, add the crushed garlic and ginger and roast for a minute.

Add the chicken mince and the soaked chana dal (split chick pea), but without any water.

Stir well.

Now add the garam masala, red chilli powder, sugar and salt.

Reduce the heat and cover the wok/pan and cook till the split chick peas become soft, but not overcooked. Otherwise, you cannot make good kebabs.

Turn off the heat source and grind the mixture in a grinder.

Take out the mixture in a bowl and add the beaten egg.

You can also add the fresh coriander leaves and the green chilli.

Knead well.

Make small patties with this mixture and keep aside.

In a non-stick pan, add the left over cooking oil and put it on your heat source.

As soon as the oil becomes hot, add the patties and gently roast on both sides.

That's all. Your delicious Chicken Shami Kebabs are ready.

Prep time: 5 minutes (in addition to the four hours required for soaking the split chick peas)

Cooking time: 25 minutes

Total time: 30 minutes

Chicken Gilauti Kebab

Traditionally made with mutton mince, this is a melt-in-the-mouth dish that was apparently "invented" to meet the demands of an old Nawab who could hardly chew. This wonderful dish can also be served as entrée. The use of chicken (instead of mutton or beef) and lentils once again improves the nutritional quotient of this dish by many notches.

Serves 3-4

Ingredients

Chicken mince-2 cup (500 grams)

Besan (Chick Pea flour) -1/2 cup (125 grams)

Onion- 1 big (chopped)

Garlic-4 cloves (crushed)

Ginger-1 inch (crushed)

Garam Masala (mixture of common Indian spices)-1/2 teaspoon

Tip: If you can't get ready-made garam masala mixture from a nearby Indian store, you can make yours by using 1 black cardamom, 3 green cardamoms, 4 cloves, and 1 inch cinnamon-all ground together for this dish.

Red Chilli Powder-1/4 teaspoon

Egg- 1 (slightly beaten)

Yoghurt unsweetened (Indian set curd is preferred) - 1/2 cup (125 grams)

 Salt- 1 teaspoon or to taste

Sugar- ¼ teaspoon

Cooking Oil-2 tablespoon

Optional: Fresh Coriander (Dhania or Cilantro) leaves- 2 tablespoon (chopped)

Green Chilli- 1 (deseeded and chopped)

Method

Marinate the chicken mince with yoghurt, crushed garlic and ginger, red chilli powder, salt, sugar and garam masala for at least 4 hours (or overnight in the fridge).

In a wok/pan, dry roast the chick pea flour till it starts giving out a nice aroma and becomes light brown. Keep it aside.

In another wok/pan, add ½ tablespoon cooking oil and put it on your heat source.

As soon as the oil becomes warm, add the chopped onion and roast till golden.

Put the mixture in a grinder and make a fine paste.

Add the roasted chick pea flour and the chicken mince with the marinade in the same grinder and grind well again.

Take out the mixture in a bowl and add the beaten egg.

You can also add the fresh coriander leaves and the green chilli.

Knead well.

Make small patties with this mixture and keep it aside.

Note: If the mixture sticks to your hand, you may keep a bowl of water and dip your hands in it occasionally. It is easier to make patties with wet hands.

In a non-stick pan, add the left over cooking oil and put it on your heat source.

As soon as the oil becomes hot, add the patties and gently roast on both sides.

That's all. Your melt-in-the-mouth Chicken Gilauti Kebabs are ready.

Prep time: 10 minutes (in addition to the four hours required for marinating the chicken mince)

Cooking time: 25 minutes

Total time: 35 minutes

Chapter 3

Chicken Curries

As any observer would readily notice, curries are quite compulsory in India.

This is so obvious that you just can't miss it. Anywhere you go and you will find curries dominating the Indian meal platter.

Why is it so, you may have wondered.

One reason could be the need to have lots of water in a tropical country like India. These curries could easily meet in a very healthy (you are boiling the water, aren't you?) and appetising manner.

The second reason could be that if you are growing so much rice you would need some curry to "wet" it, to make it less sticky and more palatable. This could be a reason that you have some kind of curries in the cuisines of all rice growing regions of the world, be it Thailand, Laos or Myanmar.

Sauces not prepared separately: It is again a very common practice in Western cuisine to boil or bake something first and then to pour on it a tomato or cheese based sauce or flambé it with some wine or such other alcoholic beverage.

In India, only restaurants semi cook their meats and vegetables and prepare some sauces separately, both to be mixed the moment someone asks for a tomato or onion or yoghurt based dish. This is because for restaurants, speed is of utmost essence. So they have to keep ingredients ready in a semi-finished condition for a quick conversion in to whatever dishes the customers demand.

However, "Home Style" (or even dhaba or wayside eatery) Indian food is made in one go with everything cooked together. The only thing to "finish" a curry dish could then be the sprinkling of some fresh Coriander (Cilantro) leaves.

With this little introduction, let me present to you 16 of the most famous "Home Style" chicken curries of India. There are in all 8 North-Indian, 3 East Indian, 2 Western, and 3 South Indian dishes. Master these and you can rustle up any other chicken dish from any part of India.

Basic Indian Chicken Curry

This is the Basic Indian Chicken Curry that once mastered can be easily adapted into a number of variations simply by adding or deleting some ingredients. It is the East Indian version from the states of Bihar and Bengal that we present here.

Serves 3-4

Ingredients

Whole chicken -1 approx. 800 grams or 28oz (4 cups) (cut into 8 pieces)

Chopped Onion-3 large

Chopped Ginger-2 inch piece

Chopped Garlic-8 Cloves

Chopped Tomatoes-3

Coriander (Dhania) powder-2 teaspoon

Turmeric powder-1 teaspoon

Garam Masala-1 teaspoon

Tip: If you can't get ready-made garam masala mixture from a nearby Indian store, you can make yours by using 1 black cardamom, 3 green cardamoms, 4 cloves, and 1 inch cinnamon-all ground together for this dish.

Red Chilli powder-1/4 teaspoon (enough only to add flavour and not to make it hot)

Cumin seeds (Jeera)-1/2 teaspoon

Tomato Ketchup-2 tablespoon

Cooking Oil-2 tablespoon

Ghee (Clarified butter)-1 tablespoon

Water-3 cups

Salt- 1 teaspoon or to taste

Method using a pressure cooker

In a pressure cooker, add the oil and put it on your heat source.

As the oil turns hot, add the cumin seeds and let them splutter.

Immediately add the chopped onion.

Stir well till the onions become translucent.

Now, add the chopped ginger and garlic and stir till all of these start giving off a nice aroma.

Add the chicken pieces and the ghee (clarified butter).

Stir well.

Add the coriander powder, turmeric, garam masala and red chilli powder.

Stir and cook the chicken till all the water evaporates and the chicken becomes almost dry. This process ensures that all the raw flavours of chicken, onions, etc. are removed.

Add now the tomatoes and the ketchup.

Stir well again and add the salt.

Let the tomatoes cook well.

Now, add the water, and close the lid of the pressure cooker with weight.

Let it come to full pressure (i.e. when the weight lifts and there is a whistling sound).

Immediately reduce the heat (to SIM on a gas stove) and let the chicken cook for 5 more minutes before turning off the heat source.

Let the cooker cool down on its own.

That's all. Your basic Indian Chicken Curry is now ready.

Method using wok/thick bottomed pan

Light the heat source and place the wok/pan on it. Add the cooking oil.

As the oil turns hot, add the cumin seeds and let them splutter.

Immediately add the chopped onion.

Stir well till the onions become translucent.

Now, add the chopped ginger and garlic and stir till all of these start giving off a nice aroma.

Add the chicken and the ghee (clarified butter).

Stir well.

Add the coriander powder, turmeric, garam masala and red chilli powder.

Stir and cook the chicken till all the water evaporates and the chicken becomes almost dry. This process ensures that all the raw flavours of chicken, onions, etc. are removed.

Add now the tomatoes and the ketchup.

Stir well again and add the salt.

Let the tomatoes cook well.

Now, add the water, and cover the wok/pan with a lid.

Reduce the heat (to SIM on a gas stove) and let the chicken cook for 20 more minutes or till the chicken becomes tender, before turning off the heat source.

That's all. Your basic Indian Chicken Curry is now ready.

Prep time: 7 minutes

Cooking time: 10 minutes with pressure cooker; 25-30 minutes with wok

Total time: 17 minutes with pressure cooker; 32-37 minutes with wok

Thick Chicken Curry

This is a tastier twist on the Basic Indian Chicken Curry that is quite popular in the East Indian states of Bihar and Bengal. The 'twist' comes from the addition of eggs and potatoes.

Serves 3-4

Ingredients

Whole chicken -1 approx. 800 grams or 28oz (4 cups) (cut into 8 pieces)

Onion-3 large (chopped)

Ginger-2 inch piece

Garlic-8 Cloves

Tomatoes-3 (chopped)

(Onion + Ginger + Garlic + Tomatoes blended and made into a fine paste)

Coriander powder-2 teaspoon

Turmeric-1 teaspoon

Garam Masala-1 teaspoon

Tip: If you can't get ready-made garam masala mixture from a nearby Indian store, you can make yours by using 1 black cardamom, 3 green

cardamoms, 4 cloves, and 1 inch cinnamon-all ground together for this dish.

Red Chilli powder-1/4 teaspoon (enough only to add flavour and not to make it hot)

Cumin seeds (Jeera)-1/2 teaspoon

Potatoes-2 (skinned and cut into big pieces)

Cooking Oil-3 tablespoon

Ghee (Clarified butter)-1 tablespoon

Water-3 cups

Egg-1

Sugar-1/2 teaspoon

Salt- 1 teaspoon or to taste

Method using a pressure cooker

In a pressure cooker, add the oil and then put it on your heat source.

As the oil turns hot, add the cumin seeds and let them splutter.

Immediately add the Onion + Ginger + Garlic + Tomatoes fine paste.

Stir well till the paste starts giving off a nice aroma and you can see the oil ooze out from the sides.

Add the chicken and stir well.

Add the coriander, turmeric, garam masala and the red chilli powder.

Cook the chicken till all the water evaporates and the chicken becomes somewhat dry.

Add the potatoes.

Stir well again and add the salt and the sugar.

Now, add the water.

Close the lid of the pressure cooker with weight and let it come to full pressure (i.e. when the weight lifts and there is a whistling sound).

Immediately reduce the heat (to SIM on a gas stove) and let the chicken cook for 5 more minutes before turning off the heat source.

Let the cooker cool down on its own.

Open the cooker and put it back on the flame.

Meanwhile, beat up the egg in a bowl.

As the curry comes to a boil, gently add the egg stirring continuously.

Remove the dish from fire.

That's all. Your Thick Chicken Curry is ready.

Method using a wok/thick bottomed pan

In a wok/pan, add the oil and then put it on your heat source.

As the oil turns hot, add the cumin seeds and let them splutter.

Immediately add the Onion + Ginger + Garlic + Tomatoes fine paste.

Stir well till the paste starts giving off a nice aroma and you can see the oil ooze out from the sides.

Add the chicken and stir well.

Add the coriander, turmeric, garam masala and red chilli powder.

Cook the chicken till all the water evaporates and the chicken is dry.

Add the potatoes.

Stir well again and add the salt and the sugar.

Now, add the water.

Cover the pan/wok with a lid, reduce the heat (to SIM on a gas stove) and let the chicken cook for 20 more minutes (or till the chicken is cooked to your liking).

Meanwhile, beat up the egg in a bowl and gently add the egg to the wok/pan stirring continuously.

Remove the dish from fire.

That's all. Your Thick Chicken Curry is ready.

Prep time: 10 minutes

Cooking time: 15 minutes with pressure cooker; 30-35 minutes in a wok

Total time: 25 minutes with pressure cooker; 40-45 minutes in a wok.

Lava Chicken or the British Tikka Masala

This is our JIFFY version of the popular Butter Chicken or the British Chicken Tikka Masala, except that we don't use any tandoor, garam masala, and also no tear-jerking onions. The bright red curry will make this dish an instant hit with the young persons in your family.

Serves 3-4

Ingredients

Whole chicken -1 approx. 800 grams or 28oz (4 cups) (cut into 8 pieces)

Yoghurt unsweetened (Indian set curd is preferred)- 3 tablespoon

Chopped Ginger-1 inch piece

Chopped Garlic-6 cloves

Coriander (Dhania) powder-1 teaspoon

Red Chilli powder-1/4 teaspoon (enough only to add flavour and not to make it hot)

Cumin (Jeera) powder-1/2 teaspoon

Salt- 1 teaspoon or to taste

For the gravy:

Chopped Tomatoes-3 large ripe

Tomato puree-200 grams (7oz) (1 cup)

Low fat fresh cream-200 grams (7oz) (1 cup)

Butter-1 tablespoon

Coriander (Dhania) powder-1 teaspoon

Cumin (Jeera) powder-1/2 teaspoon

Red Chilli powder-1/4 teaspoon (enough only to add flavour and not to make it hot)

Salt-1 teaspoon or to taste

Sugar-1 teaspoon

Cashew nuts-50 grams or 2oz or 3 tablespoon, fried golden and then chopped up. The method to fry the cashew nuts: in a small pan, add about a tablespoon of cooking oil. Put the pan on your heat source. When the oil heats up, add the cashew nuts and stir till they turn golden. Immediately remove the cashew nuts to a plate and chop. Remember, if you leave the cashew nuts in the pan, the hot oil will keep roasting the cashew nuts and may burn them.)

Method

Get the chicken ready

The first step to create this delectable dish is to make the chicken.

Method using a pressure cooker

In a pressure cooker, put the chicken pieces with all the ingredients (EXCEPT FOR THE INGREDIENTS FOR THE GRAVY).

Mix well.

Note: You can also marinate the chicken for about 2 hours in the fridge with all these ingredients as that will help the chicken become tender. However, if you are short of time, you can also make this dish right away.

Close the lid of the pressure cooker with weight and put it on your heat source.

Let the cooker come to full pressure (i.e. when the weight lifts and there is a whistling sound).

Immediately reduce the heat (to SIM on a gas stove) and let the chicken cook for 5 more minutes before turning off the heat source.

Let the cooker cool down on its own.

Method using a wok/thick bottomed pan

In a wok/pan, put the chicken pieces with all the ingredients (EXCEPT FOR THE INGREDIENTS FOR THE GRAVY).

Mix well.

Now put the wok/pan on your heat source.

Note: You can also marinate the chicken for about 2 hours in the fridge with all these ingredients as that will help the chicken become tender. However, if you are short of time, you can also make this dish right away.

When the mixture comes to a boil, reduce the heat (to SIM on a gas stove) and let the chicken cook for 20 more minutes (or till the chicken is cooked to your liking) before turning off the heat source.

How to make the gravy

Meanwhile, take a wok and put it on your heat source.

Add the butter.

When the butter melts, add the coriander, cumin and the red chilli powder.

Let the mixture roast for 1 minute.

Add the tomatoes and cook till the tomatoes soften up.

Add the tomato puree and the salt and sugar.

Gently keep stirring.

As the gravy turns a nice thick red colour, add the fresh low fat cream.

Stir well.

Switch off the heat source.

In a microwavable dish, mix together the cooked chicken and the gravy together.

Remember to add all the curry which may be there in the cooker/wok/pan as well.

Add the cashew nuts.

Microwave for 5 minutes so that all the ingredients are well integrated.

That's all. Your delicious chicken in a lava red curry with cashew nuts is ready.

Prep time: 7 minutes

Cooking time: 15 minutes with pressure cooker; 30-35 minutes in a wok; plus 5 minutes in the microwave for finishing

Total time: 27 minutes with pressure cooker; 42-47 minutes in a wok

Chicken Chettinad (Chicken cooked in a Rich Coconut Curry)

This is a classic recipe from South India that is served on special occasions in the Chettinad region of Tamilnadu. Liberal use of garam masala imparts a gourmet twist to this venerated dish.

The dish bristles with the goodness of coconut milk and coconut powder, while the typical "South Indian" taste comes from Rai (black mustard seeds) and curry leaves.

Serves 3-4

Ingredients

Whole chicken -1 approx. 800 grams or 28oz or 4 cups (cut into 8 pieces)

Onion-1 large (chopped)

Ginger-1 inch piece

Garlic-6 Cloves

Tomatoes-2 (chopped)

(Onion + Ginger + Garlic + Tomatoes blended and made into a fine paste)

Coriander (Dhania) powder-2 teaspoon

Turmeric powder-1 teaspoon

Garam Masala-1 teaspoon

Tip: If you can't get ready-made garam masala mixture from a nearby Indian store, you can make yours by using 1 black cardamom, 3 green cardamoms, 4 cloves, and 1 inch cinnamon-all ground together for this dish.

Red Chilli powder-1/4 teaspoon (enough only to add flavour and not to make it too spicy)

Coconut Milk-200 ml (1 cup approximately)

Desiccated coconut-3 tablespoon

Tamarind paste- 1 tablespoon

Black Mustard seeds (Rai) -1/2 teaspoon

Curry leaves-few (around 20)

Cooking Oil -3 tablespoon (Use a milder flavoured oil such as groundnut, sesame, or coconut for the best effect)

Salt- 1 teaspoon or to taste

Sugar- ½ teaspoon

Water-1/2 cup (roughly 150 ml)

Method using a pressure cooker

Put a pan on the heat source and DRY ROAST the desiccated coconut and the coriander powder till the coconut turns a nice golden colour.

Switch off the heat source and take out the DRY ROASTED ingredients on to a plate.

In a pressure cooker, add the oil and then put it on your heat source.

As the oil heats up, add the black mustard seeds and let them splutter.

Immediately add the Onion + Ginger + Garlic + Tomatoes fine paste.

Add the curry leaves and stir well till the paste starts giving off a nice aroma and you can see the oil ooze out from the sides.

Add the chicken pieces and stir well.

Add the turmeric, garam masala and the red chilli powder.

Cook the chicken till all the water evaporates and the chicken is rendered dry. Add the salt, sugar and DRY ROASTED desiccated coconut and coriander powder.

Stir well.

Add water.

Close the lid of the pressure cooker with weight and let it come to full pressure (i.e. when the weight lifts and there is a whistling sound).

Immediately reduce the heat (to SIM on a gas stove) and let the chicken cook for 5 more minutes before turning off the heat source.

Let the cooker cool down on its own. Open the cooker and add the coconut milk and tamarind paste.

Bring the mixture to a boil.

That's all. Your classic Chicken Chettinad is ready.

If using a thick bottomed pan or wok

Put a pan on the heat source and DRY ROAST the desiccated coconut and the coriander powder till the coconut turns a nice golden colour.

Switch off the heat source and take out the DRY ROASTED ingredients on to a plate.

Clean the pan/wok, add the oil and the put it back on your heat source.

As the oil heats up, add the black mustard seeds and let them splutter.

Immediately add the Onion + Ginger + Garlic + Tomatoes fine paste.

Add the curry leaves and stir well till the paste starts giving off a nice aroma and you can see the oil ooze out from the sides.

Add the chicken pieces and stir well. Add the turmeric, garam masala and the red chilli powder. Cook the chicken till all the water evaporates and the chicken is dry. Add the salt, sugar and DRY ROASTED desiccated coconut and coriander powder.

Stir well.

Add water.

Cover the pan/wok with a lid.

Immediately reduce the heat (to SIM on a gas stove) and let the chicken cook for 20 more minutes (or till the chicken is cooked to your liking).

Now add the coconut milk and tamarind paste.

Bring the mixture to a boil.

That's all. Your classic Chicken Chettinad is ready.

Prep time: 10 minutes

Cooking time: 20 minutes with pressure cooker; 35-40 minutes in a wok

Total time: 30 minutes with pressure cooker; 45-50 minutes in a wok

Yakhni Chicken (Yoghurt Curry)

Yakhni is a Kashmiri yoghurt based gravy dish, which is usually made with mutton. But there are vegetarian versions too using 'nadru' (lotus stem) or even the green bottle gourd (lauki). And, of course, if for reasons of health, you wish to use chicken, no one will discourage you.

Yakhni doesn't use tomatoes, turmeric or chillies. Kashmiri Pandits also don't use onions and garlic.

Kashmiris believe that Yakhni originally came from Persia, and probably reached Kashmir through the three great Moghul emperors, viz. Akbar, Jahangir, and Shahjahan, who were all so very fond of Kashmir. The earliest documented recipe is found in Ain-I-Akbari (the biography of Akbar) and is made with mutton.

Yakhni may be a corruption of Akhni, which means broth or shorba. I have tasted its Turkish version in Istanbul and was surprised to learn that it is the Turks' favourite comfort food. They call it 'Yayla Çorbası' or meadow soup. Some also call it the White soup (aks corbası), or yoghurt soup (yoğhurt corbası). All three versions are made with rice, chicken stock, egg, flour etc. which the Kashmiris don't use.

The only similarity with the Kashmiri version then is the use of yoghurt and mint.

I present here the Kashmiri version which I believe is tastier too.

Serves 3-4

Ingredients

Chicken pieces-1 Kg (2 lbs) (4 cups)

Thickly Chopped Onions large-3

Finely Sliced Onions large-2

Chopped Ginger-2 inch

Chopped Garlic-6 cloves

Brown Cardamom (Badi elaichi)-4

Cinnamon (Dalchinni)-3 one inch sticks

Yoghurt unsweetened (Indian set curd is preferred)-500 grams (20oz) (2 and 1/2 cup)

Chick pea flour (Besan)-2 tablespoon

Fennel (Saunf) powder-1/2 teaspoon

Dried Ginger powder-1/2 teaspoon

Bay Leaf (Tej patta)-4

Mint Leaves (Pudina)-15 or 20 leaves

Clarified Butter (Ghee)-1 tablespoon

Salt-1 teaspoon or to taste

Water-1 and ½ cup

Method

If using a pressure cooker

In a pressure cooker, put the chicken pieces, salt, thickly chopped onions, garlic, ginger, brown cardamom, cinnamon and water. Close the lid and place it on your heat source.

When the pressure cooker comes to full pressure, reduce the heat and cook for 5 more minutes.

Meanwhile, in a wok, beat the yoghurt and chick pea flour well with the fennel powder and dried ginger powder. Add the bay leaves.

Now place the wok on your heat source and stir till the mixture becomes almost dry.

Switch off the heat source.

Once the chicken cooks, remove the pieces from the pressure cooker to a separate plate. Take out the onion, ginger and garlic and make into a fine paste.

Add the paste and water to the yoghurt mixture in the wok. Place the wok on your heat source.

Now add the chicken pieces and the mint leaves and slow cook in the wok for about 10 minutes.

Separately in a pan, fry the finely sliced onions in the clarified butter till it takes on a nice brown colour.

Pour the onions along with the clarified butter on to the chicken dish.

That's all. Your Chicken Yakhni is ready and tastes excellent with plain rice.

If using a wok/thick bottomed pan

In a thick bottomed pan/wok, put the chicken pieces, salt, thickly chopped onions, garlic, ginger, brown cardamom, cinnamon and water. Cover with a lid and place it on your heat source.

When the mixture comes to a boil, reduce the heat and cook for 20 minutes or till the chicken becomes soft.

Meanwhile in another wok/pan, beat the yoghurt and chick pea flour well with the fennel powder and dried ginger powder. Add the bay leaves.

Now place the wok/pan on your heat source and stir till the mixture becomes almost dry.

Switch off the heat source.

Once the chicken cooks, remove the pieces from the wok/pan to a separate plate. Take out the onion, ginger and garlic and make into a fine paste.

Add the paste and water to the yoghurt mixture in the wok. Place the wok/pan on your heat source.

Add the chicken pieces and the mint leaves and slow cook in the wok/pan for about 10 minutes.

Separately in another pan, fry the finely sliced onions in the clarified butter till it takes on a nice brown colour. Pour the onions along with the clarified butter on to the chicken dish.

That's all. Your Yakhni Chicken is ready and tastes excellent with plain rice.

Prep time: 5 minutes

Cooking time: 25 minutes with pressure cooker, 45 minutes with deep pan/wok

Total time: 30 minutes with pressure cooker, 50 minutes with deep pan/wok.

Chicken Korma (Chicken in a Mughlai White Curry)

This is a classic preparation from North India that claims its heritage from the days of the Mughals. The dish uses NO chillies, red or green, and so can be served to people of all ages who would like a somewhat 'safer' introduction to Indian cuisine.

Serves 3-4

Ingredients

Chicken pieces-1 Kg (2 lbs) (4 cups)

Onions chopped finely-500 grams (18oz) (2 cups)

Garlic chopped-8 cloves

Ginger chopped-2 inch piece

Green Cardamom (Chhoti Elaichi)-4

Brown Cardamom (Badi Elaichi)-2

Cinnamon (Dalchinni)-1 inch stick

Cloves (Laung)-6

Bay Leaves (Tejpatta)-2

Cumin Seeds (Jeera)-1 teaspoon

Cashew nuts-3 tablespoon

Blanched Almonds-3 tablespoon

Raisins-3 tablespoon

(Cashew nuts + Almonds + Raisins to be blended into a fine paste)

Desiccated coconut-2 tablespoon

Fresh cream-1/2 cup

Yoghurt unsweetened (Indian set curd is preferred)-200 grams (8oz) 1 cup

Cooking Oil-2 tablespoon

Clarified Butter (ghee)-2 tablespoon

Salt- 1 teaspoon or to taste

Water-2 cups

Method

Method using a pressure cooker

Light up your heat source and place the pressure cooker on it. Add the cooking oil and the ghee together.

As soon as the oil heats up, add the cardamom, bay leaves, cinnamon, cloves and the cumin seeds (Jeera). Let them brown for a few seconds.

Add the onions and roast till the onions become translucent. Add the garlic and ginger and let them roast for a few minutes.

Add the chicken pieces and fry well.

Now add the dry fruits (Cashew nuts + Almonds + Raisins) paste and again roast. Add the desiccated coconut and yoghurt.

Stir till all the water has evaporated. Now add the salt and water and close the lid.

Let the cooker come to full pressure. Reduce the heat (to SIM on a gas stove) and let it cook for 5 more minutes.

Switch off the heat source and let the cooker cool before opening it.

After opening the cooker, add the fresh cream and serve your delicious Chicken Korma.

Method using wok/thick bottomed pan

Light the heat source and place the wok/pan on it. Add the cooking oil and the ghee together.

As soon as the oil heats up, add the cardamom, bay leaves, cinnamon, cloves and the cumin seeds (jeera). Let them brown for a few seconds.

Add the onions and roast till the onions become translucent. Add the garlic and ginger and let them roast for a few minutes.

Add the chicken pieces and fry well.

Now add the dry fruits (Cashew nuts + Almonds + Raisins) paste and again roast. Add the desiccated coconut and yoghurt.

Stir till all the water has evaporated. Now add the salt and water and cover the wok/pan with a lid.

Reduce the heat and let it cook. Keep checking the chicken to see that there is enough water and that the chicken is not getting burnt. If required, add more water. Cook till the chicken becomes tender which should take approximately 20 minutes.

Switch off the heat source and add the fresh cream.

That's all. Your delicious Chicken Korma is ready.

Prep time: 10 minutes

Cooking time: 20 minutes with pressure cooker; 35 minutes with a wok/pan

Total time: 30 minutes with pressure cooker; 45 minutes with a wok/pan

Khubani Murg (Chicken with Apricots)

This is a Kashmiri gravy dish, which is usually made with mutton. But if for reasons of health, you wish to use chicken, I'm sure no one will discourage you.

Serves 3-4

Ingredients

Chicken pieces-1 Kg (2 lbs) (4 cups) or Whole chicken -1 (cut into 8 pieces)

Chopped Onion-3 large

Chopped Ginger-2 inch piece

Chopped Garlic-8 Cloves

Chopped Tomatoes-3

Turmeric (Haldi) powder-1 teaspoon

Garam Masala-1 teaspoon

Tip: If you can't get ready-made garam masala mixture from a nearby Indian store, you can make yours by using 1 black cardamom, 3 green cardamoms, 4 cloves, and 1 inch cinnamon-all ground together for this dish.

Red Chilli powder-1/4 teaspoon (enough only to add flavour and not to make it hot)

Cumin (Jeera) seeds-1/2 teaspoon

Saffron strands- 8 or ½ teaspoon (dissolved in 2 tablespoon hot water)

Dried apricots (Khubani) - 1 cup (soaked overnight and deseeded)

Tomato Ketchup-2 tablespoon

Cooking Oil-2 tablespoon

Ghee (Clarified butter)-1 tablespoon

Water-1 cup

Salt- 1 teaspoon or to taste

Method using a pressure cooker

In a pressure cooker, add the oil and the put it on your heat source.

As the oil heats up, add the cumin seeds and let them splutter.

Immediately add the chopped onion.

Stir well till the onions become translucent.

Now, add the chopped ginger and garlic and stir till these start giving off a nice aroma.

Add the chicken and the ghee (clarified butter).

 Stir well.

Add the turmeric powder, garam masala and the red chilli powder.

Stir and cook the chicken till all the water evaporates and the chicken becomes almost dry. This process ensures that all the raw flavours of chicken, onions, etc. are removed.

Add now the tomatoes and the ketchup.

Stir well again and add the salt.

Let the tomatoes cook well.

Add the soaked apricots and the saffron strands along with the water the saffron was soaked in.

Now, add the water, and close the lid of the pressure cooker with weight.

Let it come to full pressure (i.e. when the weight lifts and there is a whistling sound).

Immediately reduce the heat (to SIM on a gas stove) and let the chicken cook for 5 more minutes before turning off the heat source.

Let the cooker cool down on its own.

That's all. Your Khubani Murg or Chicken with Apricots is now ready.

Method using a wok/thick bottomed pan

Light the heat source and place the wok/pan on it. Add the cooking oil.

As the oil heats up, add the cumin seeds and let them splutter.

Immediately add the chopped onion.

Stir well till the onions become translucent.

Now, add the chopped ginger and garlic and stir till these start giving off a nice aroma.

Add the chicken and the ghee (clarified butter).

Stir well.

Add the turmeric powder, garam masala and the red chilli powder.

Stir and cook the chicken till all the water evaporates and the chicken becomes almost dry. This process ensures that all the raw flavours of chicken, onions, etc. are removed.

Add now the tomatoes and the ketchup.

Stir well again and add the salt.

Let the tomatoes cook well.

Add the soaked apricots and the saffron strands along with the water the saffron was soaked in.

Now, add the water, and cover the wok/pan with a lid.

Reduce the heat (to SIM on a gas stove) and let the chicken cook for 20 more minutes or till the chicken becomes tender, before turning off the heat source. In case, you find the dish becoming too dry, you may add ½ a cup of water.

That's all. Your Khubani Murg or Chicken with Apricots is now ready.

Prep time: 7 minutes

Cooking time: 10 minutes with pressure cooker; 25-30 minutes with wok

Total time: 17 minutes with pressure cooker; 32-37 minutes with wok

Murg Mattar (Chicken Green Pea Curry)

Want to infuse the goodness of legumes into your chicken dish? Then try this unique recipe from Northern India and attain nutritional Nirvana.

Serves 3-4

Ingredients

Chicken pieces-1 Kg (2 lbs) (4 cups) or Whole chicken -1 (cut into 8 pieces)

Chopped Onion-3 large

Chopped Ginger-2 inch piece

Chopped Garlic-8 Cloves

Desiccated Coconut – 2 tablespoon

Turmeric (Haldi) powder-1 teaspoon

Garam Masala-1 teaspoon

Tip: If you can't get ready-made garam masala mixture from a nearby Indian store, you can make yours by using 1 black cardamom, 3 green cardamoms, 4 cloves, and 1 inch cinnamon-all ground together for this dish.

Red Chilli powder-1/4 teaspoon (enough only to add flavour and not to make it hot)

Cumin (Jeera) seeds-1/2 teaspoon

Lemon juice- 1 tablespoon

Chopped Fresh Coriander (Dhania) leaves- 2 tablespoon

Green peas (shelled fresh are preferred) --200 grams (7oz) (1 cup)

Cooking Oil-2 tablespoon

Ghee (Clarified butter)-1 tablespoon

Water-1 cup

Salt- 1 teaspoon or to taste

Method using a pressure cooker

In a pressure cooker, add the oil and then put it on your heat source.

As the oil heats up, add the cumin seeds and let these splutter.

Immediately add the chopped onion.

Stir well till the onions become translucent.

Now, add the chopped ginger and garlic and stir till these start giving off a nice aroma.

Add the chicken and the ghee (clarified butter).

 Stir well.

Add the turmeric powder, garam masala and the red chilli powder.

Stir and cook the chicken till all the water evaporates and the chicken becomes almost dry. This process ensures that all the raw flavours of chicken, onions, etc. are removed.

Add now the desiccated coconut and green peas.

Stir well again and add the salt.

Now, add the water, and close the lid of the pressure cooker with weight.

Let it come to full pressure (i.e. when the weight lifts and there is a whistling sound).

Immediately reduce the heat (to SIM on a gas stove) and let the chicken cook for 5 more minutes before turning off the heat source.

Let the cooker cool down on its own.

Before serving, add the lemon juice and the fresh coriander (cilantro).

That's all. Your Murg Mattar or Chicken Green Pea Curry is now ready.

Method using a wok/thick bottomed pan

Light the heat source and place the wok/pan on it. Add the cooking oil.

As the oil heats up, add the cumin seeds and let these splutter.

Immediately add the chopped onion.

Stir well till the onions become translucent.

Now, add the chopped ginger and garlic and stir till these start giving off a nice aroma.

Add the chicken and the ghee (clarified butter).

Stir well.

Add the turmeric powder, garam masala and the red chilli powder.

Stir and cook the chicken till all the water evaporates and the chicken becomes almost dry. This process ensures that all the raw flavours of chicken, onions, etc. are removed.

Add now the desiccated coconut and green peas.

Stir well again and add the salt.

Now, add the water, and cover the wok/pan with a lid.

Reduce the heat (to SIM on a gas stove) and let the chicken cook for 20 more minutes or till the chicken becomes tender before turning off the heat source. In case, you find the dish becoming too dry, you may add ½ a cup of water.

Before serving, add the lemon juice and the fresh coriander (cilantro).

That's all. Your Murg Mattar or Chicken Green Pea Curry is now ready.

Prep time: 7 minutes

Cooking time: 10 minutes with pressure cooker; 25-30 minutes with wok

Total time: 17 minutes with pressure cooker; 32-37 minutes with wok

Chicken in a Coconut Curry

This is a South Indian style, chicken recipe. If you have had only North Indian style chicken so far, try this finger-licking good recipe with such exotic flavours that they will wow you over.

Ingredients

Whole chicken -1 approx. 800 grams or 28oz or 4 cups (cut into 8 pieces)

Onion-1 large (chopped)

Ginger-1 inch piece

Garlic-6 Cloves

Tomatoes-2 (chopped)

(Onion + Ginger + Garlic + Tomatoes blended and made into a fine paste)

Coriander (Dhania) powder-2 teaspoon

Turmeric (Haldi) powder-1 teaspoon

Garam Masala-1 teaspoon

Tip: If you can't get ready-made garam masala mixture from a nearby Indian store, you can make yours by using 1 black cardamom, 3 green cardamoms, 4 cloves, and 1 inch cinnamon-all ground together for this dish.

Red Chilli powder-1/4 teaspoon (enough only to add flavour and not to make it spicy)

Black Mustard seeds (Rai)-1/2 teaspoon

Curry leaves- 10-12

Coconut Milk-400 ml (1 + ½ cups)

Potatoes-2 (skinned and cut into small pieces)

Cooking Oil-3 tablespoon

Salt- 1 teaspoon or to taste

Method using a pressure cooker

In a pressure cooker, add the oil and then put it on your heat source.

As the oil turns hot, add the black mustard seeds and let them splutter.

Immediately add the Onion + Ginger + Garlic + Tomatoes fine paste.

Add the curry leaves and stir well till the paste starts giving off a nice aroma and you can see the oil ooze out from the sides.

Add the chicken pieces and stir well.

Add the coriander, turmeric, garam masala and red chilli powder.

Cook the chicken till all the water evaporates and the chicken is somewhat dry.

Add the potatoes. Stir well again.

Now add the coconut milk and salt.

Close the lid of the pressure cooker with weight and let it come to full pressure (i.e. when the weight lifts and there is a whistling sound).

Immediately reduce the heat (to SIM on a gas stove) and let the chicken cook for 5 more minutes before turning off the heat source.

Let the cooker cool down on its own.

That's all.

Your Chicken in Coconut Milk is ready.

Method using a wok/pan

In a wok/pan, add the oil and then put it on your heat source.

As the oil turns hot, add the black mustard seeds and let them splutter.

Immediately add the Onion + Ginger + Garlic + Tomatoes fine paste.

Add the curry leaves and stir well till the paste starts giving off a nice aroma and you can see the oil ooze out from the sides.

Add the chicken and stir well.

Add the coriander, turmeric, garam masala and red chilli powder.

Cook the chicken till all the water evaporates and the chicken is somewhat dry.

Add the potatoes. Stir well again.

Now add the coconut milk and salt.

Cover the pan/wok with a lid, reduce the heat (to SIM on a gas stove) and let the chicken cook for 20 more minutes (or till the chicken is cooked to your liking) before turning off the heat source.

That's all.

Your Chicken in Coconut Milk is ready.

Prep time: 10 minutes

Cooking time: 15 minutes with pressure cooker; 30-35 minutes in a wok

Total time: 25 minutes with pressure cooker; 40-45 minutes in a wok

Murg Badami (Chicken Almond Curry)

This is a gourmet dish that you may rarely find even in a 5-star restaurant. Attempt this, therefore, only in a somewhat relaxed frame of mind. Use of almonds and saffron make this a very different (and somewhat expensive) dish.

Serves 4

Ingredients

Whole chicken -1 approx. 800 grams or 28oz or 4 cups (cut into 8 pieces)

Chopped Onion-3 large

Sliced Onions- 2 large

Chopped Ginger-2 inch piece

Chopped Garlic-8 Cloves

Chopped Tomatoes-3

Coriander (Dhania) powder-2 teaspoon

Turmeric (Haldi) powder-1 teaspoon

Fennel (Saunf) - ½ teaspoon (ground)

Poppy seeds (Khaskhas) - 1 teaspoon (ground)

Garam Masala-1 teaspoon

Tip: If you can't get ready-made garam masala mixture from a nearby Indian store, you can make yours by using 1 black cardamom, 3 green cardamoms, 4 cloves, and 1 inch cinnamon-all ground together for this dish.

Red Chilli powder-1/4 teaspoon (enough only to add flavour and not to make it hot)

Cumin (Jeera) seeds-1/2 teaspoon

Saffron (Kesar) strands- ½ teaspoon (dissolved in two tablespoon hot water)

Tomato Ketchup-2 tablespoon

Yoghurt unsweetened (Indian set curd is preferred)- 200 grams (8oz) 1 cup (water drained)

Almonds- ½ cup (blanched)

Cooking Oil-2 tablespoon

Ghee (Clarified butter)-1 tablespoon

Water-2 cups

Salt- 1 and ½ teaspoon or to taste

Method using a pressure cooker

Heat the oil and ghee together in a pressure cooker and fry the two sliced onions till they turn golden-brown.

Take out the onions and keep aside.

As the oil/ghee would still be hot, add the cumin seeds and let them splutter.

Immediately add the three chopped onions.

Stir well till the onions become translucent.

Now, add the chopped ginger and garlic and stir till these start giving off a nice aroma.

Add the chicken pieces.

Stir well.

Add the coriander powder, turmeric powder, fennel powder, garam masala and red chilli powder.

Stir and cook the chicken till all the water evaporates and the chicken becomes almost dry. This process ensures that all the raw flavours of chicken, onions, etc. are removed.

Add now the tomatoes and the ketchup.

Stir well again and add the salt.

Let the tomatoes cook well.

Now, add the poppy seeds, blanched almonds, and the saffron strands.

Stir well.

Add the water, and close the lid of the pressure cooker with weight.

Let it come to full pressure (i.e. when the weight lifts and there is a whistling sound).

Immediately reduce the heat (to SIM on a gas stove) and let the chicken cook for 5 more minutes before turning off the heat source.

Let the cooker cool down on its own.

Open the pressure cooker, add the yoghurt and the fried onions.

Put the pressure cooker back on your heat source and simmer the mixture for about two minutes, uncovered.

That's all. Your exotic Murg Badami (Chicken Almond Curry) is now ready.

Method using wok/thick bottomed pan

Heat the oil and ghee together in a pan/wok and fry the two sliced onions till they turn golden-brown.

Take out the onions and keep aside.

In the same wok/pan, now add the cumin seeds and let them splutter.

Immediately add the three chopped onions.

Stir well till the onions become translucent.

Now, add the chopped ginger and garlic and stir till they start giving off a nice aroma.

Add the chicken pieces.

Stir well.

Add the coriander powder, turmeric powder, fennel powder, garam masala and red chilli powder.

Stir and cook the chicken till all the water evaporates and the chicken becomes almost dry. This process ensures that all the raw flavours of chicken, onions, etc. are removed.

Add now the tomatoes and the ketchup.

Stir well again and add the salt.

Let the tomatoes cook well.

Now, add the poppy seeds, blanched almonds, and the saffron strands.

Stir well.

Add the water, and cover the wok/pan with a lid.

Immediately reduce the heat (to SIM on a gas stove) and let the chicken cook for 20 more minutes (or till the chicken is cooked to your liking).

Now add the yoghurt and the fried onions, and let the mixture simmer for about two minutes, uncovered.

That's all. Your exotic Murg Badami (Chicken Almond Curry) is now ready.

Prep time: 10 minutes

Cooking time: 15 minutes with pressure cooker; 35-40 minutes with wok

Total time: 25 minutes with pressure cooker; 45-50 minutes with wok

Murg Kali Mirch (Chicken with Cashew and Black Pepper)

This is a "white curry" dish that the young in your family may find tastier. Combine this with a Chicken Shami Kebab or Chicken Tikkas and you will have a party going.

Serves 3-4

Ingredients

Whole chicken -1 approx. 800 grams or 28oz (4 cups) (cut into 8 pieces)

Yoghurt unsweetened (Indian set curd is preferred)- 100 grams (4oz) 1/2 cup; Hung

Note- To make hung curd, put two cups of unsweetened yoghurt in a muslin cloth and hang it over a bowl for about 2-3 hours. This will help drain away the excess water.

Chopped Ginger-1 inch piece

Chopped Garlic-6 cloves

Coriander (Dhania) powder-1 teaspoon

Red Chilli powder-1/4 teaspoon (enough only to add flavour and not to make it spicy)

Cumin (Jeera) powder-1/2 teaspoon

Garam Masala (mixture of common Indian spices) crushed- 1/2 tea spoon

Tip: If you can't get ready-made garam masala mixture from a nearby Indian store, you can make yours by using 1 black cardamom, 3 green cardamoms, 4 cloves, and 1 inch cinnamon-all ground together for this dish.

Salt- 1 teaspoon or to taste

For the gravy:

Low fat fresh cream-400 grams (14oz) (2 cup)

Butter-1 tablespoon

Salt- ½ teaspoon

Sugar- ½ teaspoon

Cashew nuts- 1 cup (crushed)

Black Pepper- 1 tablespoon (crushed)

Method

Get the chicken ready

The first step to create this delectable dish is to make the chicken.

Method using a pressure cooker

In a pressure cooker, put the chicken pieces with all the ingredients (EXCEPT FOR THE INGREDIENTS FOR THE GRAVY).

Mix well.

Note: You can also marinate the chicken for about 2 hours in the fridge with all these ingredients as that will help the chicken become tender. However, if you are short of time, you can also cook right away.

Close the lid of the pressure cooker with weight and put it on your heat source.

Let the cooker come to full pressure (i.e. when the weight lifts and there is a whistling sound).

Immediately reduce the heat (to SIM on a gas stove) and let the chicken cook for 5 more minutes before turning off the heat source.

Let the cooker cool down on its own.

Method using wok/thick bottomed pan

In a wok/pan, put the chicken pieces with all the ingredients (EXCEPT FOR THE INGREDIENTS FOR THE GRAVY).

Mix well.

Now put the wok/pan on your heat source.

Note: You can also marinate the chicken for about 2 hours in the fridge with all these ingredients as that will help the chicken become tender. However, if you are short of time, you can also cook right away.

When the mixture comes to a boil, reduce the heat (to SIM on a gas stove) and let the chicken cook for 20 more minutes (or till the chicken is cooked to your liking) before turning off the heat source.

Now make the gravy

Meanwhile, take a wok and put it on your heat source.

Add the butter.

When the butter melts, add the crushed cashew nuts and roast for about two minutes.

Now add the fresh cream, salt, and sugar, and bring the mixture to a boil while stirring continuously.

Switch off the heat source.

In a microwavable dish, mix together the cooked chicken and the gravy.

Sprinkle the crushed black pepper.

Remember to add all the curry which may be there in the cooker/wok/pan.

Microwave for 5 minutes so that all the ingredients are well integrated.

That's all. Your delicious Murg Kali Mirch (Chicken with Cashew and Black Pepper) is ready.

Prep time: 7 minutes

Cooking time: 10 minutes with pressure cooker; 30 minutes in a wok; plus 5 minutes in the microwave for finishing

Total time: 22 minutes with pressure cooker; 42 minutes in a wok

Chicken Keema Mattar (Chicken Mince-Peas Curry)

This is yet another dish that infuses the goodness of legumes into your chicken, and helps you attain nutritional Nirvana in a JIFFY.

Serves 3-4

Ingredients

Chicken mince--1/2 Kg (500 grams or 18oz or 2 cups)

Green peas (shelled fresh are preferred) --200 grams (7oz) (1 cup)

Medium size Onions--2 (chopped)

Garlic-4 pieces

Ginger-1 inch

Fresh tomato-2 (chopped)

Turmeric (Haldi) - 1/2 tea spoon

Dry crushed coriander (Dhania)-2 tea spoon

Garam Masala (mixture of common Indian spices) crushed- 1/2 tea spoon

Tip: If you can't get ready-made garam masala mixture from a nearby Indian store, you can make yours by using 1 black cardamom, 3 green

cardamoms, 4 cloves, and 1 inch cinnamon-all ground together for this dish.

Kashmiri Red Chilli powder--1/4 tea spoon (Recommended for colour, but if you like your dish to be really spicy, use any other red chilli powder)

Yoghurt unsweetened (Indian set curd is preferred)-1 table spoon

Cumin whole (Jeera)-1/2 tea spoon

Salt-1/2 tea spoon (or to taste)

Tomato Ketchup-1 table spoon

Cooking oil-1 table spoon

Ghee (clarified butter)-1 tea spoon

Water-1 tea cup

Method using a pressure cooker

Blend together (in a blender preferably!) the onions, garlic, ginger and tomatoes to a fine paste.

Heat the oil in a pressure cooker.

Add cumin seeds to the oil and as they turn brown, add the paste from the blender and gently fry.

As the paste starts giving off a nice aroma, add the chicken mince and sauté gently.

Add all the dry garam masala, salt and curd to this mixture and keep stirring on low flame (SIM on a gas stove) till they start becoming almost dry.

Add the Ketchup and peas to the mixture and stir again.

At this juncture, add the Ghee for a lovely taste.

Add the water, close the lid with weight and bring it to full pressure on high flame.

Reduce the heat (to SIM on a gas stove), and cook for 3 minutes. Let the cooker cool down on its own before opening it.

That's all.

Your Chicken Keema Matar is ready.

Method using a wok/pan

Blend together (in a blender preferably!) the onions, garlic, ginger and tomatoes to a fine paste.

Heat the oil in a wok/pan.

Add cumin seeds to the oil and as these turn brown, add the paste from the blender and gently fry.

As the paste starts giving off a nice aroma, add the chicken mince and sauté gently.

Add all the dry garam masala, salt and curd to this mixture and keep stirring on low flame (SIM on a gas stove) till they start becoming almost dry.

Add the Ketchup and peas to the mixture and stir again.

At this juncture, add the Ghee for a lovely taste.

Add the water, and let the mixture come to a boil.

Cover the wok/pan with a lid, reduce the heat (to SIM on a gas stove), and cook for 20 minutes (or till the chicken is cooked to your taste).

That's all.

Your Chicken Keema Matar is ready.

Prep time: 7 minutes

Cooking time: 10 minutes with pressure cooker; 20 minutes with a wok/deep pan

Total time: 17 minutes with pressure cooker; 27 minutes with a wok/deep pan

Chicken Kofta (Chicken Mince Ball) Curry

Kofta is basically a meatball (in this case a chicken meat ball) that is made with chicken mince, egg, garam masala, salt and bread slices.

The chicken kofta curry is just another variation of the famous Indian chicken curry.

Serves 3-4

Ingredients

Chicken mince -1/2 Kg (18oz) (2 cups)

Onion-2 large (chopped)

Ginger-2 inch piece

Garlic-8 Cloves

Tomatoes-3 (chopped)

(Onion + Ginger + Garlic + Tomatoes blended and made into a fine paste)

Coriander (Dhania) powder-2 teaspoon

Turmeric (Haldi) powder-1 teaspoon

Garam Masala-1+1/2 teaspoon

Tip: If you can't get ready-made garam masala mixture from a nearby Indian store, you can make yours by using 2 black cardamom, 4 green

cardamoms, 6 cloves, and 1.5 inch cinnamon-all ground together for this dish.

Red chilli powder-1/4 teaspoon (enough only to add flavour and not to make it hot)

Cumin (Jeera) seeds-1/2 teaspoon

Cooking Oil-3 tablespoon

Ghee (Clarified butter)-1 tablespoon

Water-3 cups

Bread-2 slices soaked in water

Egg-1

Sugar-1/2 teaspoon

Salt- 1 and ½ teaspoon or to taste

Method

In a bowl, mix together the chicken mince, one egg, half teaspoon garam masala and half teaspoon salt.

Add the bread slices after squeezing out all the water.

Make into walnut size balls.

In a frying pan, add the cooking oil and gently fry these balls 2-3 at a time and keep them aside on a plate.

Switch off the heat source.

Method using a pressure cooker

In a pressure cooker, pour the oil from the pan and put it on your heat source.

As the oil turns hot, add the cumin seeds and let them splutter.

Immediately add the Onion + Ginger + Garlic + Tomatoes fine paste.

Stir well till the paste starts giving off a nice aroma and you can see the oil ooze out from the sides.

Add the coriander powder, turmeric, remaining 1 spoon of garam masala and red chilli powder.

Stir well again and add one teaspoon salt and the sugar.

Now, add the water.

As the mixture comes to a boil, gently add the fried chicken balls.

Close the lid of the pressure cooker with weight and let it come to full pressure (i.e. when the weight lifts and there is a whistling sound).

Immediately reduce the heat (to SIM on a gas stove) and let the chicken balls cook for 2 more minutes before turning off the heat source.

Let the cooker cool down on its own.

That's all.

Your delicious Chicken Kofta Curry is ready.

Method using a wok/pan

In another wok/pan, pour the oil from the pan (after frying the meatballs) and put it on your heat source.

As the oil turns hot, add the cumin seeds and let them splutter.

Immediately add the Onion + Ginger + Garlic + Tomatoes fine paste.

Stir well till the paste starts giving off a nice aroma and you can see the oil ooze out from the sides.

Add the coriander powder, turmeric, remaining 1 spoon of garam masala and red chilli powder.

Stir well again and add one teaspoon salt and the sugar.

Now, add the water.

As the mixture comes to a boil, gently add the fried chicken balls.

Cover the wok/pan with a lid, reduce the heat (to SIM on a gas stove) and let the chicken balls cook for 10 minutes before turning off the heat source.

That's all.

Your delicious Chicken Kofta Curry is ready.

Prep time: 10 minutes

Cooking time: 10 minutes with pressure cooker; 20 minutes with a wok

Total time: 20 minutes with pressure cooker; 30 minutes with a wok

Chicken Rishta (Chicken Mince Ball in a saffron sauce) Curry

Rishta is a popular Kashmiri dish that is traditionally made with boneless mutton cubes that are pounded with wooden mallets for hours by expert Kashmiri wazas (cooks) till they acquire their typical spongy texture.

For reasons of health as well as convenience, we present here a variation that is made with chicken mince.

Ingredients

Chicken mince -1/2 Kg (18oz) (2 cups)

Arrowroot powder- 2 tablespoon

Onion-2 large (chopped)

Ginger-2 inch piece (chopped)

Tomato puree- 2 tablespoon

Turmeric (Haldi) powder-1 teaspoon

Black cardamom (Badi Elaichi) - 2

Green cardamoms (Chhoti Elaichi) -4

Cloves (Laung) - 4

Cinnamon (Dalchini) - 1 inch (2.5 cm)

Red Chilli powder-1/2 teaspoon (enough only to add flavour and not to make it spicy)

Cooking Oil-1 tablespoon

Ghee (Clarified butter)-1 tablespoon

Water-2 cups

Saffron (Kesar) -1/2 teaspoon (dissolved in 2 tablespoon hot water)

Salt- 1 and ½ teaspoon or to taste

Method

In a bowl, mix together the chicken mince, arrowroot powder and half teaspoon salt.

Make into egg size balls.

In a wok/pan, add the water, turmeric and the chilli powder and put it on your heat source.

As the mixture comes to a boil, gently add the chicken balls.

Cover the wok/pan with a lid, reduce the heat (to SIM on a gas stove) and let the chicken balls cook for 10 minutes before turning off the heat source.

In another wok/pan, add the oil and the ghee, and put it on your heat source.

When the oil heats up, add the whole spices, the chopped onion and the chopped ginger.

Stir well till the onions become translucent.

Add the tomato puree and 1 teaspoon salt.

Stir well again.

Now, add the chicken balls along with the water/stock these were cooked in to this wok/pan.

Add the dissolved saffron and bring to a boil.

That's all.

Your delicious Chicken Rishta (Chicken in a Saffron Sauce) is ready.

Prep time: 10 minutes

Cooking time: 20 minutes

Total time: 30 minutes

Chicken Vindaloo

This is a dish from Goa, the land of eternal sand, surf and beach parties in Western India. The name and the use of vinegar shows a little bit of Portuguese influence on this dish.

Serves 3-4

Ingredients

Whole chicken -1 approx. 800 grams or 28oz or 4 cups (cut into 8 pieces)

Chopped Ginger-2 inch piece (chopped)

Chopped Garlic-8 Cloves

Garam Masala-1 teaspoon

Tip: If you can't get ready-made garam masala mixture from a nearby Indian store, you can make yours by using 1 black cardamom, 3 green cardamoms, 4 cloves, and 1 inch cinnamon-all ground together for this dish.

Red Chilli powder-1 teaspoon (enough only to add flavour and not to make it too hot)

Cumin (Jeera) seeds-1 teaspoon

Black Mustard Seeds (Rai) - 1 teaspoon

Vinegar- ½ cup

Cooking Oil-2 tablespoon

Water-3 cups

Salt- 1 teaspoon or to taste

Method

In a wok/deep pan, add the oil and put it on your heat source.

As the oil heats up, add the cumin and black mustard seeds and let them splutter.

Immediately add the chopped ginger and garlic and stir till it starts giving off a nice aroma.

Add the garam masala and the red chilli powder.

Now pour in the vinegar and the chicken pieces.

Stir well again and add the salt.

 Switch off the heat source and let the chicken stand for about an hour to marinate.

Now switch on the heat source again and simmer the chicken till tender.

Keep stirring occasionally so that nothing sticks to the bottom or burns.

That's all. Your Chicken Vindaloo is now ready.

Prep time: 7 minutes

Cooking time: 25 minutes (excluding the one hour for marination)

Total time: 32 minutes (excluding the one hour for marination)

Goan Chicken Xacuti

Pronounced Shaquti, this is another dish from Goa, Western India that is bristling with Portuguese influence. The exotic flavours are guaranteed to take your breath away. Try only when you are in a mood for adventure and are NOT too rushed.

Serves 3-4

Ingredients

Whole chicken -1 approx. 800 grams or 28oz or 4 cups (cut into 8 pieces)

Chopped Onion-1

Chopped Ginger- 1 teaspoon

Chopped Garlic-1 teaspoon

Coriander (Dhania) powder-1/2 teaspoon

Green Cardamoms (Chhoti Elaichi) - 2

Cloves (Laung) - 2

Cinnamon (Dalchinni) - ½ inch (1 cm.)

Turmeric (Haldi) powder- 1 teaspoon

Whole Red Chillies- 2 (deseeded to add flavour and not to make it too hot; you can add more if you desire a really spicy dish.)

Cumin (Jeera) seeds-1/2 teaspoon

Desiccated coconut- ½ cup

Poppy seeds (Khaskhas) - 3 teaspoons

Fenugreek (Methi) seeds- ½ teaspoon

Water-1/2 cup

Salt- 1 teaspoon or to taste

Black Pepper- 1 teaspoon (whole)

Cooking Oil- 2 tablespoon

Ghee- 1 tablespoon

Lemon juice- 1 tablespoon

Method

Place a pan over your heat source and dry roast the coriander and cumin seeds till they start changing colour and giving out a nice aroma.

Remove to a plate.

In the same pan, add the fenugreek seeds and the black pepper (whole) and roast for 2-3 minutes.

Remove to the same plate.

The same way, now roast the poppy seeds and the desiccated coconut till the latter attain a golden brown colour.

Remove to the same plate.

Now dry roast the chopped onions till brown.

Note: All the above have to be roasted separately, in batches, because they all have different roasting points. If you roast them all together, some may get burnt while others may NOT be that well-roasted.

Now put all the ingredients, except the chicken, lemon juice and the cooking oil, in a blender and blend well with a little (2 tablespoon) water.

Using a Pressure Cooker

If you have a pressure cooker, put it on your heat source, and pour in the cooking oil and the ghee.

When the oil heats up, add the blended mixture and fry till the oil separates to the sides.

Now add the chicken pieces and mix well.

Fry till the chicken is almost dry.

Now add the water, and close the lid of the pressure cooker with weight.

Let it come to full pressure (i.e. when the weight lifts and there is a whistling sound).

Immediately reduce the heat (to SIM on a gas stove) and let the chicken cook for 5 more minutes before turning off the heat source.

Let the cooker cool down on its own.

Open the pressure cooker and add the lemon juice.

That's all. Your exotic Goan Chicken Xacuti is ready.

Method using the wok/pan

If you wish to use a wok/pan, put it on your heat source, and pour in the cooking oil and the ghee. When the oil heats, add the blended mixture and fry till the oil separates to the sides. Now add the chicken pieces and mix well. Fry till the chicken is almost dry.

Now add the water, and cover the wok/pan with a lid.

Immediately reduce the heat (to SIM on a gas stove) and let the chicken cook for 20 more minutes (or till it is cooked to your liking) before turning off the heat source.

You may need to add some more water if the gravy becomes too thick and starts sticking to the vessel.

Now add the lemon juice.

That's all. Your exotic Goan Chicken Xacuti is ready.

Prep time: 20 minutes (including the dry roast time)

Cooking time: 10 minutes with pressure cooker; 25 minutes with a wok

Total time: 30 minutes with pressure cooker; 45 minutes with a wok

Chapter 4

The Raj Effect

Imagine the bewilderment of the British who land up in India in the 17th century to discharge their "white man's burden" of civilizing the natives. Proud of their clothes, weaponry, language and culture, they first encountered the Maharajas and their fabulous palaces whose wealth and opulence made the English royalty feel like paupers. And then at royal repasts, they were bombarded with so many strange spices and flavours that went much beyond the simple salt and pepper that were more or less the only "spice" they were accustomed to back home.

But to the credit of the British, they never gave up. They adapted the humble Indian dal (lentil curry) to substitute for their soups. They introduced baking and the use of cheese. They got Indians to grow all kinds of European vegetables like cauliflower, cabbage, bell peppers and even potato.

The "fusion" recipes that thus evolved under the British Raj were initially preserved and passed on by the Khansamas (cooks) of Clubs, Government Dak Bungalows, Circuit Houses or State Guest Houses scattered all over India. Now quite a number of restaurants and hotels carry out these traditions with great pride and aplomb.

In that background, we present eight chicken gems from the days of the Raj. These are mostly continental recipes but with an Indian twist.

Enjoy!

Chicken Chops

This dish uses garam masala and is more suited for dinners than snacks. Most clubs prefer to make this dish with either chicken or mutton mince, as they are more easily available, which makes this quite a rare gourmet dish.

Serves 3-4

Ingredients

Boiled Chicken mince- 250 grams (9oz) (1 cup)

Onions (chopped) - 2

Ginger (chopped) - 1 teaspoon

Garlic (chopped) - 1 teaspoon

Green Chillies (deseeded and finely chopped) - 2

Black Pepper (crushed) - ¼ teaspoon

Cumin seeds (Jeera) - ½ teaspoon

Garam Masala- ½ teaspoon

Tip: If you can't get ready-made garam masala mixture from a nearby Indian store, you can make yours by using 1 black cardamom, 3 green cardamoms, 4 cloves, and 1 inch cinnamon-all ground together for this dish.

Tomato ketchup- 1 tablespoon

Fresh Coriander (Cilantro) leaves (finely chopped) - 2 tablespoon

Raisins- 1 tablespoon

Salt- 1/4 teaspoon or to taste

Cooking oil- 1 tablespoon

For the covering:

Potatoes (boiled and mashed) - 1/2 Kg (18oz) (2 cups)

Salt and pepper to taste

Egg-1

Wheat flour- 2 tablespoon

Bread crumbs- ½ cup

Water- 1/4 cup

AND

Cooking Oil (enough to deep fry) - depends on the size of your wok/deep frying pan

Method

Place a pan on your heat source and put one tablespoon of cooking oil.

As soon as the oil heats up, add the cumin seeds.

In a few seconds the cumin will splutter and brown. Immediately add the chopped onion, garlic and ginger.

Sauté till these start changing colour and giving off a nice aroma.

Now add the boiled chicken mince and rest of the ingredients. Mix well and cook for about 2 minutes.

Switch off the heat source.

Meanwhile take the mashed potatoes and add salt and pepper.

Take two tablespoon of this mixture in your hands and make a hole in the middle.

Fill the hole up with the chicken mixture and roll into an egg shape.

Make sure that the chicken mixture is covered well with the potato on all sides.

Repeat till all the chicken is thus shaped.

Now make the coating

In another bowl, break an egg and mix together with the wheat flour and water well.

In a plate, spread the bread crumb.

Take out one piece of chicken chop at a time, and dip it into the egg-flour mixture.

Then take the chicken chop out and gently roll it on the plate with breadcrumbs so that it is evenly coated.

Do this with all the chicken chops.

Heat oil in a frying pan or wok.

Take 2 chicken chops and gently slide into the hot oil.

Gently turn them around and take out from the oil when they are nice and golden brown.

Remove to a plate and add the next batch to the oil.

Repeat till all the chicken chops are fried.

Please ensure that the chops do not burn.

Your Chicken Chops are ready.

If using an Air Fryer

Pre-heat the Air Fryer at 200 degree C (392 degrees F) for 5 minutes.

Follow all the preparatory steps listed above till you come to deep frying in oil.

Now, with a silicon brush, gently brush the coated chicken chops with a little oil on all sides.

Place the chicken chops in the Air Fryer in a way that all pieces remain separate and NOT on top of one another.

Air-fry for 8 minutes at 200 degree C (392 degrees F).

Repeat till all the chicken chops are air-fried.

Prep time: 20 minutes; Plus 5 minutes if using the Air Fryer

Cooking time: 2 minutes @ each batch for wok/pan; 8 minutes@ each batch for Air Fryer

Total time: Approximately 40 minutes for wok/pan; 65 minutes for Air Fryer

Chicken Bell Pepper (Capsicum)

This recipe in a rare flourish uses garam masala with capsicum (bell pepper), which no Chinese would ever dare attempt. But we are talking about the British here, aren't we?

Serves 3-4

Ingredients

Boiled Chicken mince- 250 grams (9oz) (1 cup)

Bell Peppers (Capsicum) - 4 (cut in half with seeds removed)

Onions (chopped) - 2

Ginger (chopped) - 1 teaspoon

Garlic (chopped) - 1 teaspoon

Black Pepper (crushed) - ¼ teaspoon

Cumin Seeds (Jeera) - ½ teaspoon

Garam Masala- ½ teaspoon

Tip: If you can't get ready-made garam masala mixture from a nearby Indian store, you can make yours by using 1 black cardamom, 3 green cardamoms, 4 cloves, and 1 inch cinnamon-all ground together for this dish.

Tomato ketchup- 1 tablespoon

Fresh Coriander (Cilantro) leaves (finely chopped) - 2 tablespoon

Raisins- 1 tablespoon

Salt- 1/4 teaspoon or to taste

Cooking oil- 1 tablespoon

Method

Place a pan on your heat source and put one tablespoon of cooking oil.

As soon as the oil heats up, add the cumin seeds.

In a few seconds the cumin will splutter and brown. Immediately add the chopped onion, garlic and ginger.

Sauté till these start changing colour and gives off a nice aroma.

Now add the chicken mince and rest of the ingredients. Mix well and cook for about 2 minutes.

Switch off the heat source.

Switch on the oven.

While the oven pre-heats, take the bell pepper halves and stuff them with the chicken filling.

Place these on a baking tray and bake for 10 minutes at 200 degree C (392 degrees F).

That's all. Your Chicken Bell Peppers are ready.

Prep time: 25 minutes

Cooking time: 20 minutes

Total time: Approximately 45 minutes

Making Cold Chicken

This is a real party dish. You will not be able to resist the taste of chicken in white sauce, combined with the taste of fresh cream and fresh/canned fruits, and served chilled.

Although the dish doesn't use any traditional Indian ingredients, the Khansamas (cooks) of old Dak Bungalows and Circuit Houses always credit the British for introducing this dish to India.

Are you then ready to make this exotic dish? Then let's begin.

Serves 3-4

Ingredients

Whole chicken -1 approx. 800 grams or 28oz or 4 cups (cut into 8 pieces)

Wheat flour–2 tablespoon

Milk-500 ml (2 cups approximately)

Grated Cheese Cheddar-50 grams (2oz) (3 tablespoon)

Fresh Cream (Low fat)–200 grams (1 cup)

Canned mixed fruit–1 small can

Apple-1

Cucumber-1

Black grapes to decorate- 100 grams (1/2 cup)

Butter-1 teaspoon

Salt-1 teaspoon or to taste

Sugar-1 teaspoon

Water- 250 ml (1 cup approximately)

Method

Put 1 cup water in a pressure cooker/pan and submerge the chicken in that water.

If using a pressure cooker, put it on your heat source and let the cooker come to full pressure.

Immediately reduce the heat (to SIM on a gas stove) and cook for 5 minutes. Switch off.

If using a pan, put it on your heat source and let the water start boiling.

Immediately reduce the heat and let the chicken simmer for about 10 minutes.

It is advised that you check that the chicken has been cooked properly. This can be done by using a fork to prick the chicken to see whether it has become quite tender.

Take the pan off from the heat source.

Once the water cools down, take the chicken out from the pressure cooker/pan and put it on a plate.

Note: Save the stock (water that you used for boiling the chicken) for making soups or any other dish later. If you don't want to do that, then you can just keep boiling the water and 'dry' the chicken in your pressure cooker/pan.

Now make the white sauce

Put a pan on your heat source and add the butter.

After the butter melts, add the flour.

Gently mix the flour with the butter making sure that the flour does NOT turn brown.

Switch off the heat source and let the flour cool down.

When it comes to room temperature, gently add the milk (also at room temperature) and mix well to ensure that no lumps are formed.

Return this to your heat source, add the cheese and a pinch of salt.

As soon as the mixture thickens, your white sauce is ready.

Ready the Dish

In a bowl, whisk the fresh cream with a pinch of salt.

To this mixture, add the canned fruit and the chopped up apple and the cucumber.

In a big serving dish, place the chicken in the middle, each piece separately and pour the white sauce over it. Put the mixed fruit all along the sides and decorate with the black grapes.

That's all. Your delicious Cold Chicken is ready.

You can eat it at room temperature if it is very cold or cool it in the fridge before serving if the weather is hot.

Prep time: 10 minutes

Cooking time: 17 minutes

Total time: 27 minutes

The Original KFC-style Indian Fried Chicken

While very few people in the world know exactly what was in Colonel Sanders' mix of 11 secret herbs and spices, that went on to make the famous Kentucky Fried Chicken, two facts are clear. One, that he used a pressure cooker; and two, that there are some Indian spices among those 11 herbs.

KFC claims to be keeping Colonel Sanders' original handwritten recipe locked away in a vault. But it is interesting to note that the Colonel had complained many times in his life that KFC had stopped using his original recipe.

In fact, Sanders was quoted, in 1970 by the New Yorker, saying that KFC's new gravy recipe "ain't fit for my dogs."

While I'd reserve my judgment on the issue of taste, let me share with you a much tastier version of the KFC from the time of the British Raj, which you can very easily rustle up in the comforts of your own home.

Ingredients for preparing the Chicken

Whole chicken -1 approx. 800 grams or 28oz (4 cups) (cut into 8 pieces)

Chopped Onion-1

Chopped Ginger- 1 teaspoon

Chopped Garlic-1 teaspoon

Coriander (Dhania) powder-1/2 teaspoon

Black Cardamom (Badi Elaichi) - 1

Green Cardamoms (Chhoti Elaichi) - 2

Cloves (Laung) - 2

Cinnamon (Dalchinni) - ½ inch (1 cm.)

Red Chilli powder-1/4 teaspoon (enough only to add flavour and not to make it hot)

Cumin seeds (Jeera) -1/2 teaspoon

Water-1 cup (250 ml)

Salt- 1 teaspoon or to taste

Black Pepper- ½ teaspoon (ground)

Ingredients for the coating

Bread crumbs- 2 cups

Egg-2

Arrowroot or Corn Flour-1/2 cup dissolved in a cup of water

Salt- 1/4 teaspoon or to taste

Cooking oil- enough for deep frying (quantity depends on the size of your pan/wok)

Method

Boil the chicken with all the ingredients listed for preparing the chicken.

This should take about 5 minutes in a pressure cooker, after the cooker comes to full pressure.

In a wok/pan, this may take about 20 minutes.

Take the chicken out once the water has cooled.

Note: Save the stock (water that you used for boiling the chicken) for making soups or any other dish later. If you don't want to do that, then you can just keep boiling the water and 'dry' the chicken in your pressure cooker/pan.

Prepare the Coating

While your chicken cooks in the pressure cooker/wok/pan, break the eggs in a bowl.

Pour in the dissolved arrowroot/corn flour mixture.

Add the salt and mix well.

Let this sit for about 15 minutes.

In another plate, spread the bread crumbs.

Take out the cooked chicken pieces (after they have cooled), one by one and coat them first in the egg and arrowroot/corn flour mixture and then coat with the bread crumbs.

Keep aside.

Put a pan/wok on your heat source and pour in enough cooking oil to deep fry the chicken.

When the oil heats up, put in your coated chicken pieces one-by-one.

Gently turn over the pieces till the chicken pieces are golden brown all over.

Remove these to a plate covered with a paper napkin to absorb the excess oil.

That's all. Your Original KFC-style Indian Fried Chicken is ready.

Method using an Air Fryer

If you have ever fancied having a KFC style chicken but without the fat and calories, you have to use an Air Fryer. Here you then air fry (or bake) a breaded chicken instead of deep frying. At least to me, the results were excellent and the taste was not really compromised. In fact, I have had some very positive feedback from people who tried this recipe at home.

So, if you want to minimise the use of oil, and have access to an Air fryer, you should first set the Air Fryer to pre-heat for 5 minutes at 200 degree Celsius (392 degrees F).

While the Air-Fryer preheats, brush each coated chicken piece with a little cooking oil and place it in the Air Fryer (after it is pre-heated), ensuring that pieces don't cover each other.

Now air-fry for 10 minutes at 200 degree Celsius (392 degrees F).

Repeat till all the chicken pieces are done.

That's all. Your Original KFC-style Indian Air Fried Chicken is ready.

Prep time: 10 minutes

Cooking time: 15 minutes with pressure cooking and deep frying; 25 minutes with boiling in a wok/pan and deep frying.

Note: For air frying, you will have to add 20 more minutes.

Total time: 25 minutes with pressure cooking and deep frying; 35 minutes with boiling in a wok/pan and deep frying.

Grilled Chicken

Trust the British to come up with a really healthy way to have dinner, and that too without using a grill.

This recipe assumes that you have removed the skin of the chicken, which is where all the bad fat and cholesterol resides.

Serves 3-4

Ingredients

Whole chicken -1 approx. 800 grams or 28oz (4 cups) (cut into 8 pieces)

Lemon juice-2 tablespoon

White Vinegar-2 tablespoon

Chopped garlic-8 cloves

Salt- 1 teaspoon or to taste

Black Pepper ground- ½ teaspoon or to taste

Butter-3 tablespoon

Method

Marinate the chicken pieces with all the ingredients except the butter.

Let the chicken marinate for about two hours at room temperature (or overnight in the fridge).

Now put a non-stick pan on your heat source and add the butter.

When the butter melts, put the chicken pieces, in batches, in the pan and let them sizzle.

When the pieces start changing colour (that is when the raw look goes away, a whitish colour appears, before the chicken turns golden brown), gently turn them to the other side using a fork. In this way, you gently grill the chicken pieces on both sides on low heat.

If the chicken still doesn't look cooked, add half cup water and cover the pan with a lid.

Remove the lid after two minutes and turn the pieces.

Do this till all the water evaporates and your chicken looks nicely cooked and crisp on the outside.

Please make sure that the heat is low and the chicken doesn't burn.

That's all. Your delicious Grill Chicken is ready.

Prep time: 5 minutes (excluding marination)

Cooking time: 25 minutes

Total time: 30 minutes

Shepherd's Pie

This is a classic British dish which some of the Dak Bungalows in India can rustle up only if you give them some advance notice. The original recipe uses mutton mince, but for reasons of health, there is no problem if you insist on the use of chicken mince.

Serves 2-3

Ingredients

Potatoes-5

Bread slices-2 (soaked in water)

Note: Bread slices soak water immediately; so don't soak for long.

Chicken Mince-1 cup

Chopped Onion Large-1

Garlic-4 cloves

Ripe Tomatoes-2

Grated Cheese-2 tablespoon

Egg-1

Cinnamon (Dalchinni) stick-1 inch

Black Pepper ground-1/4 teaspoon

Chilli flakes-1/4 teaspoon

Butter/Cooking Oil-2 tablespoon

Salt- ½ teaspoon or to taste

Method

Boil, peel and mash the potatoes.

Squeeze the water out of the bread slices and add.

Mix the grated cheese, egg and salt with the mashed potato and keep aside.

In a wok/deep pan, add the butter and put it on your heat source.

As soon as the butter melts, add the garlic cloves.

The garlic cloves will soon start giving out a nice aroma.

Then add the chopped onion.

Sauté till the onions become translucent.

Now add the mince and stir well.

Roast the mince till it changes colour and becomes almost dry.

Now add the tomatoes, cinnamon, pepper, chilli flakes and salt to taste.

Stir till the tomatoes are well cooked.

Switch off the heat source.

Take a baking tray and cover the bottom and the sides of the tray with half the mashed potato mixture.

Pour the cooked mince on top of this.

Cover with another layer of the mashed potato mixture.

Bake in the oven for about 10 minutes at 150 degrees C (302 degrees F) or till the potatoes get a nice golden colour.

That's all. Your Shepherd's Pie is ready.

Prep time: 10 minutes

Cooking time: 20-25 minutes

Total time: 30-35 minutes

Chicken Cheese Cream with Spinach

This is one of my favourite dishes. I owe my love for spinach to this recipe. When chicken juice, cheddar cheese, spinach and cream blend together, the taste is really out of this world.

Serves 3-4

Ingredients

Whole chicken -1 approx. 800 grams or 28oz (4 cups) (cut into 8 pieces) WITHOUT SKIN

Spinach-2 Kgs (4.4lb) (8 cups)

Lemon juice-2 Lemons

White Vinegar-2 tablespoon

Salt- 1 teaspoon or to taste

Black Pepper ground- to taste

Cheddar Cheese-100 grams (4oz) (half cup)

Fresh low fat cream-200 grams (7oz) (1 cup)

Fresh bread slices -4 (crumbled without toasting the bread)

Water-4 cups

Cooking Oil-2 tablespoon

Feel free to add any other seasonings of your choice that you think should be added to this dish.

Method

Marinate the chicken pieces with salt, vinegar and lemon juice for at least 4 hours (at room temperature).

Wash and chop up the spinach.

 In a vessel, bring the water to a boil and add the spinach. Let it boil once again.

Drain the water and press the spinach till all the water is taken out.

In a big baking dish (approx. 20 cm by 20 cm or 8 inches by 8 inches) place the spinach.

Add a tablespoon of cream, some salt and pepper and make it the base.

In a pan, add the cooking oil and put it on your heat source. When it warms up, fry the chicken pieces in batches. The chicken should turn into a nice golden brown colour. Do regulate your heat source to ensure that your chicken doesn't burn.

Place these lightly fried chicken on top of the spinach base and pour the remaining cooking oil on top of it.

Cover the chicken with low fat cream followed by the grated cheese.

Sprinkle the bread crumbs over this.

Place it in the microwave and cook on high for 10 minutes.

The chicken will get cooked in this time but to crisp/brown the chicken and to help the flavours blend, place it in the oven (or use the grill option of your microwave, if it has one) for another 10 minutes.

You can also bake this dish in a conventional oven (without using a microwave) but then it will take 30-40 minutes (instead of the 20 minutes in the combo-method described above) to be ready.

This is a complete dish, but you can always use some plain rice or bread to go with this.

Prep time: 10 minutes

Cooking time: 20 minutes in microwave and 40 minutes in oven

Total time: 30 minutes in microwave and 50 minutes in oven

Honey Orange Chicken

This is an extremely delicious and low calorie recipe. The sweetness and zest of orange with the subtle saltiness of chicken breast is really appetising and soothing to your soul.

Serves 3-4

Ingredients

Chicken breast boneless-4

Honey-4 teaspoon

Orange juice non-sweetened-2 cup

Orange zest-2 tablespoon (Take the skin of an orange and scrape off the white portion. The skin then forms the zest.)

Garlic-8 cloves crushed

Chilli flakes-1 teaspoon

Salt- 1 teaspoon or to taste

Cooking oil-1 tablespoon

Butter-1 tablespoon

Spring Onions (chopped up along with leaves)-8

Method

In a pan, heat the cooking oil and butter together.

Add the chicken breasts after sprinkling some salt on it.

Roast well on both sides till the chicken breasts become light brown.

Meanwhile, in a bowl mix together the honey, orange juice, orange zest, garlic, chilli flakes and rest of the salt.

Add this mixture to the chicken breasts and let these cook till the chicken becomes nice and soft and the sauce thickens.

Turn off the flame and then add the spring onions.

That's all. Your Honey Orange Chicken is ready.

This dish really goes well with Sauté vegetables and roasted baby potatoes.

Prep time: 10 minutes

Cooking time: 15 minutes

Total time: 25 minutes

Chapter 5

Cooking Eggs—The Indian Way

What's so great about cooking eggs, is a legitimate question. After all, who can't boil, fry, scramble or poach an egg? And if you can do all these, certainly churning out a mean omelette should also be not very difficult.

Well, trust the Indians then to once again complicate such a simple recipe as boiled eggs into an absolutely exotic Nargisi Kofta. Or, to cook the same boiled eggs with coconut to turn into a delicious Kerala-style curry.

Or, to give a fiery Parsi or Marathi twist to your poor scrambled eggs and omelettes.

The permutations can be just breathlessly endless!

We present in that background a selection of just eight Indian recipes which use eggs in a way which is interesting and quite mouth-watering.

Chicken Nargisi Kofta (dry)

This is an exotic take on the British Devil that can be enjoyed as a snack, entrée or as a part of a dinner.

Serves 3-4

Ingredients

Hard boiled eggs- 6 (peeled)

Chicken mince-2 cup (500 grams)

Chana Dal (Split Chick Pea) -1/2 cup (125 grams); soaked in water for at least 4 hours

Chopped Garlic-4 cloves

Chopped Ginger-1 inch

Garam Masala (mixture of common Indian spices)-1/2 teaspoon

Tip: If you can't get ready-made garam masala mixture from a nearby Indian store, you can make yours by using 1 black cardamom, 3 green cardamoms, 4 cloves, and 1 inch cinnamon-all ground together for this dish.

Red Chilli Powder-1/4 teaspoon

Egg- 1 (slightly beaten)

Salt- 1 teaspoon or to taste

Sugar- ¼ teaspoon

Cooking Oil- enough to deep fry (quantity depends on the size of your wok/pan)

Method

In a wok/pan, add ½ tablespoon cooking oil and put it on your heat source.

As soon as the oil becomes warm, add the crushed garlic and ginger and roast for a minute.

Add the chicken mince and the soaked chana dal (split chick pea) both without the water.

Stir well.

Now add the garam masala, red chilli powder, sugar and salt.

Reduce the heat and cover the wok/pan and cook till the split chick peas become soft but not overcooked. Otherwise, you cannot make good patties.

Turn off the heat source and grind the mixture in a grinder.

Take out the mixture in a bowl and add the beaten egg.

Knead well.

Take one boiled (and peeled) egg at a time and cover it with this mixture.

Press with your hands so that the mixture sticks to the egg well.

Keep aside.

In a wok/deep pan, add some cooking oil and put it on your heat source.

As soon as the oil becomes hot, add the egg patties, one by one, and gently fry till golden.

Remove with a slotted spoon to a paper napkin to absorb the excess oil.

That's all.

Your exotic Chicken Nargisi Koftas (dry) are ready.

Prep time: 10 minutes (in addition to the four hours required for soaking the split chick peas)

Cooking time: 25 minutes

Total time: 35 minutes

Egg Potato Curry

This is a handy dish for the days when you don't have access to any fresh green vegetables. The protein of the eggs is balanced with the carbs from the potatoes and the curry lets you enjoy this dish with a portion of just plain boiled rice.

Serves 3-4

Ingredients

Egg-6 Hard boiled and peeled

Potatoes-2 boiled and cut into pieces

Chopped Onion-1

Chopped Ginger-1 inch

Chopped Garlic-4 cloves

Chopped Tomatoes-3

Garam Masala-1/2 teaspoon

Tip: If you can't get ready-made garam masala mixture from a nearby Indian store, you can make yours by using 1 black cardamom, 3 green cardamoms, 4 cloves, and 1 inch cinnamon-all ground together for this dish.

Turmeric powder (Haldi)-1/2 teaspoon

Red Chilli powder -1/4 teaspoon (This quantity only adds some flavour but does not make the food hot. You may add more if you so prefer.)

Tomato Ketchup-1 tablespoon

Cooking Oil-2 tablespoon

Water-1 cup

Salt- 1 teaspoon or to taste

Method

In a blender, blend together the chopped onion, ginger, garlic and tomatoes and make into a fine paste.

In a wok, add the cooking oil and put it on your heat source.

When the oil becomes hot, add the hard boiled eggs and fry gently.

Remove the eggs from oil and keep them on a plate.

Add the onion+ ginger + garlic +tomato paste to the same oil.

Fry well till you get a nice aroma from the paste.

Add the rest of the ingredients and stir well.

Now, add the eggs, boiled potatoes with a cup of water and salt.

When this mixture comes to a boil, turn off the heat source.

That's all. Your delicious Egg Potato Curry is ready.

Prep time: 10 minutes

Cooking time: 10 minutes

Total time: 20 minutes

Mootey Molee (Kerala Egg and Coconut Curry)

This is a dish from the verdant coasts of Kerala that transforms the humble boiled eggs into a really flavourful recipe.

Serves 3-4

Ingredients

Egg-6 Hard boiled and peeled

Onion-1 large (chopped)

Ginger-1 inch piece (chopped)

Garlic-6 Cloves (chopped)

Turmeric powder-1 teaspoon

Fresh Green Chillies- 2 (deseeded and sliced, enough only to add flavour and not to make it spicy)

Curry leaves- 10-12

Coconut Milk-400 ml (1 + ½ cups)

Cooking Oil-2 tablespoon

Salt- 1 teaspoon or to taste

Lemon juice- 1 teaspoon

Method

In a wok/pan, add the oil and then put it on your heat source.

As the oil turns hot, add the onion, ginger, garlic, green chillies, and the curry leaves. Stir well till the onions become translucent.

Add the turmeric powder, coconut milk and salt.

Now add the boiled eggs and let them simmer uncovered for ten minutes.

Switch off the heat source and add the lemon juice.

That's all.

Your flavourful Mootay Molee (Kerala Egg and Coconut Curry) is ready.

Prep time: 10 minutes (including the time for boiling eggs)

Cooking time: 15 minutes

Total time: 25 minutes

Akoori- Scrambled Eggs the Parsi Way

If you ever wanted to turn your simple scrambled eggs into something more exotic, just try out this Parsi dish. The recipe is as far away from Persian cuisine as are the current days Parsis living in Mumbai are from Iran!

Serves 4-5

Ingredients

Chopped Onion-2

Chopped Ginger- 1 teaspoon

Red or Green Chilli fresh-2 (deseeded and chopped)

Chopped Tomato- 1

Eggs-8

Milk- 4 tablespoon

Salt- ¾ teaspoon or to taste

Ground Black Pepper- ½ teaspoon or to taste

Turmeric powder- 1/8 teaspoon

Ground Cumin seeds- ½ teaspoon

Butter or Ghee-2 tablespoon

Optional: Fresh Coriander (Cilantro) leaves- 1 tablespoon chopped

Method

In a bowl, beat up the eggs well with milk, salt and pepper.

In a non-stick pan, add the butter/ghee and put it on your heat source.

As soon as the butter/ghee warm up, add the chopped onion, ginger and chillies.

Stir well till the onions become translucent.

Add the turmeric powder, tomato and the ground cumin seeds and fry for a minute.

Pour the eggs over this mixture and gently keep stirring.

Let the eggs cook for a while till they acquire a wet but creamy consistency.

Please ensure that the mixture doesn't become too dry.

Switch off the heat source.

Sprinkle the chopped fresh coriander, if you so wish, before serving.

Prep time: 5 minutes

Cooking time: 5 minutes

Total time: 10 minutes

Palak-Omelette (Eggs with Spinach)

If you ever wanted to infuse the goodness of spinach in to a humble breakfast dish, try out this Indian version. Then show Popeye Cartoons to your kids, and let them turn into lifelong worshippers of spinach.

Serves 3-4

Ingredients

Spinach- (Only leaves)-1 cup

Chopped Onion-1

Chopped Ginger- 1 teaspoon

Red Chilli Powder- ¼ teaspoon (just for colour, use more if you want it really hot)

Chopped Garlic- 1 teaspoon

Eggs-6

Salt- ¾ teaspoon or to taste

Ground Black Pepper- ½ teaspoon or to taste

Cumin seeds (Jeera) - ½ teaspoon

Butter or Ghee-1 tablespoon

Method

Wash and chop the spinach.

In a vessel, bring the water to a boil and add the spinach. Boil once again.

Drain the water and press the spinach till all the water is taken out.

In a bowl, beat up the eggs well with salt and pepper. Keep aside.

In a non-stick pan, add the butter/ghee and put it on your heat source.

As soon as the butter/ghee warm up, add the cumin seeds and let them splutter.

Now add the chopped onion, garlic, and ginger.

Stir well till the onions become golden.

Now add the spinach and the red chilli powder and fry for a minute.

Pour the eggs over this mixture and let the eggs cook for a while till they set.

Take a plate and gently slide the omelette on it.

Prep time: 10 minutes (including chopping and boiling spinach)

Cooking time: 5 minutes

Total time: 15 minutes

Chicken Nargisi Kofta Curry

Want to know how your British Devils would taste in a curry? Then try this Indian version, and you would sure be asking for more.

Serves 3-4

Ingredients

Hard boiled eggs- 6 (peeled)

Chicken mince-2 cup (500 grams)

Chana Dal (Split Chick Pea) -1/2 cup (125 grams); soaked in water for at least 4 hours

Chopped Garlic-4 cloves

Chopped Ginger-1 inch

Garam Masala (mixture of common Indian spices)-1/2 teaspoon

Tip: If you can't get ready-made garam masala mixture from a nearby Indian store, you can make yours by using 1 black cardamom, 3 green cardamoms, 4 cloves, and 1 inch cinnamon-all ground together for this dish.

Red Chilli Powder-1/4 teaspoon

Egg- 1 (slightly beaten)

Salt- 1 teaspoon or to taste

Sugar- ¼ teaspoon

Cooking Oil- enough to deep fry (quantity depends on the size of your wok/pan)

For the gravy:

Chopped Tomatoes-3 large ripe

Tomato puree-200 grams (7oz) (1 cup)

Low fat fresh cream-200 grams (7oz) (1 cup)

Butter-1 tablespoon

Coriander (Dhania) powder-1 teaspoon

Cumin (Jeera) powder-1/2 teaspoon

Red Chilli powder-1/4 teaspoon (enough only to add flavour and not to make it spicy)

Salt-1 teaspoon

Sugar-1 teaspoon

Method for making the Koftas

In a wok/pan, add ½ tablespoon cooking oil and put it on your heat source.

As soon as the oil heats up, add the crushed garlic and ginger and roast for a minute.

Add the chicken mince and the soaked chana dal (split chick pea) both without the water.

Stir well.

Now add the garam masala, red chilli powder, sugar and salt.

Reduce the heat and cover the wok/pan and cook till the split chick peas become soft but not overcooked. Otherwise, you cannot make good patties.

Turn off the heat source and grind the mixture in a grinder.

Take out the mixture in a bowl and add the beaten egg.

Knead well.

Take one boiled egg at a time and cover it with this mixture.

Press with your hands so that the mixture sticks to the egg well.

Keep aside.

In a wok/deep pan, add some cooking oil and put it on your heat source.

As soon as the oil becomes hot, add the egg patties, one by one, and gently fry till golden.

Remove with a slotted spoon to a paper napkin to absorb the excess oil.

Now make the gravy

Take another wok and put it on your heat source.

Add the butter.

When the butter melts, add the coriander, cumin and the chilli powder.

Let the mixture roast for 1 minute.

Add the tomatoes and cook till the tomatoes soften up.

Add the tomato puree and the salt and sugar.

Gently keep stirring.

As the gravy turns a nice thick red colour, add the fresh low fat cream.

Stir well.

Switch off the heat source.

Now make the Nargisi Kofta Curry

Slice the Nargisi Koftas in half and place them in a microwavable dish.

Pour the gravy over the koftas.

Microwave for 5 minutes so that all the ingredients are well integrated.

That's all. Your delicious Nargisi Kofta Curry is ready.

Prep time: 10 minutes (in addition to the four hours required for soaking the split chick peas)

Cooking time: 35 minutes

Total time: 45 minutes

Parsi Poro (Marathi Omelette)

Here is the spicy twist to your humble omelette from the land of the Marathas. Although credited to the Parsis, the recipe has almost nothing in common with the egg preparations that the Persians make in modern Iran today.

Serves- 2

Ingredients

Potatoes- 1 cup diced

Chopped Onion-1

Fresh Green or Red Chillies-2 (deseeded and chopped)

Eggs-4

Salt- ¾ teaspoon or to taste

Ground Black Pepper- ¼ teaspoon or to taste

Ground Cumin (Jeera) Seeds- ½ teaspoon

Cooking Oil-1 tablespoon

Butter-1 tablespoon

Fresh Coriander (Cilantro) leaves- 1 tablespoon chopped

Method

Boil the potatoes till they become a little soft but not totally cooked. Peel and dice the potatoes into small cubes.

In a non-stick pan, add the cooking oil and butter.

As soon as the oil and butter warm up, add the potatoes.

Fry till they are light brown.

Remove with a slotted spoon and keep aside.

Please ensure that there are no potato residues as the same pan will be used now to make the omelette.

In a bowl, beat up the egg whites separately till they stiffen.

Now add the egg yolks, cumin seeds powder, salt and pepper. Mix well.

Now add the chopped onion, coriander and chillies.

Put the pan back on the heat source.

As the oil heats, pour in the egg mixture.

Let the eggs cook for a while till they set.

Sprinkle the fried potatoes and fold the egg.

Take a plate and gently slide the folded omelette on it.

Prep time: 5 minutes

Cooking time: 10 minutes

Total time: 15 minutes

Omelette-with an Indian twist

If you are looking for a less spicy Indian-style omelette than the Parsi Paro, try this variation. The recipe also has some additional greens in the shape of green peas.

Serves- 1

Ingredients

Potatoes-2

Shelled Peas-1 tablespoon

Chopped Onion-1

Chopped Garlic- 2 cloves

Chilli Flakes-1/4 teaspoon

Tomato puree- 1 tablespoon

Eggs-2

Salt and Pepper to taste

Cooking Oil-1 tablespoon

Butter-1 tablespoon

Optional: Fresh Coriander (Cilantro) leaves- 1 tablespoon chopped

Method

Boil the potatoes till they become a little soft but not totally cooked. Peel and cut the potatoes into thin slices.

In a non-stick pan, add the cooking oil and butter.

As soon as the oil and butter warm up, add the potatoes. Roast well.

Add the chopped onion, garlic, peas, tomato puree and chilli flakes. Let them all cook together till the potatoes are done. Sprinkle a little salt.

Meanwhile beat up the eggs well with salt and pepper.

Pour the egg over the onion, peas and potato mixture in the non-stick pan.

Let the eggs cook for a while till they set.

Take a plate and gently slide the omelette on it.

Sprinkle the chopped fresh coriander, if you so wish, before serving.

Prep time: 5 minutes

Cooking time: 10 minutes

Total time: 15 minutes

Chapter 6

Chicken Cooked with Rice

If you are looking to have a complete meal centred on chicken, try cooking it up with rice, the Indian way. The Biryani, Pilaf or just fried rice thus achieved would be absolutely delicious.

Rice is a great neutral medium to cook all kinds of meats with. We present five basic recipes, which once mastered can be used to rustle up myriad variations.

Chicken Biryani

Biryanis are normally elaborate affairs with saffron-tinged rice layered with cooked meats, lots of ghee and then cooked in a pot sealed with dough. We present here, however, our Home- Style JIFFY version, which is in my opinion also tastier and healthier.

Ingredients

For the chicken:

Whole chicken -1 approx. 800 grams or 28oz (4 cups) (cut into 8 pieces)

Chopped Onion-3 large

Chopped Ginger-2 inch piece

Chopped Garlic-8 Cloves

Tomatoes-2

Yoghurt unsweetened (Indian set curd is preferred)-1 table spoon

Coriander (Dhania) powder-2 teaspoon

Garam Masala-1 teaspoon

Tip: If you can't get ready-made garam masala mixture from a nearby Indian store, you can make yours by using 1 black cardamom, 3 green cardamoms, 4 cloves, and 1 inch cinnamon-all ground together for this dish.

Red Chilli powder-1/4 teaspoon (enough only to add flavour and not to make it hot)

Cumin seeds (Jeera)-1/2 teaspoon

Cooking Oil-2 tablespoon

Ghee (Clarified butter)-1 tablespoon

Water- 5-6 cups (just to ensure that the chicken cooks well and doesn't burn)

Salt- 1 teaspoon or to taste

For the rice:

Long grain rice (Basmati)-2 cups

Chicken stock-4 cups (Please use the same cup that you used for measuring the rice.)

Black Cumin seeds (Shahi Jeera)-1/2 teaspoon

Green Cardamom (Chhoti elaichi)-4

Brown Cardamom (Badi elaichi)-2

Cinnamon (Dalchini)-1 inch

Cloves (Laung)-6

Bay leaf (Tejpatta)-1

Clarified butter (Ghee)-1 tablespoon

Salt to taste

Sugar-1/2 teaspoon

Few strands of saffron dissolved in ¼ cup warm milk

Blanched Almonds-24 kernels

(To blanch almonds, immerse them in half a cup of hot water for 30 minutes. Remove the skin thereafter.)

Method

First of all, wash the rice well (in a vessel 3-4 times, but don't rub it lest the grains break) and let it naturally "dry", on an inclined plate, for 15-20 minutes. This helps enhance the aroma.

Next, prepare the chicken stock. Put in a vessel, the neck and wings of the chicken and pour 4 cups of water over it. Now add ½ inch piece of cinnamon, one green cardamom, and two cloves.

If using pressure cooker, cook under full pressure for 5 minutes.

If not using a pressure cooker, then let the stock be made for half an hour in a wok/deep pan on low heat.

Remove the chicken pieces, strain and keep the stock ready.

Method to prepare the chicken using a pressure cooker

In a pressure cooker, add the oil and then put it on your heat source.

As the oil turns hot, add the cumin seeds and let them splutter.

Immediately add the chopped onion.

Stir well till the onions become translucent.

Now, add the chopped ginger and garlic and stir till they start giving off a nice aroma.

Add the chicken and the ghee (clarified butter).

Stir well.

Add the coriander powder, garam masala and the red chilli powder.

Stir and cook the chicken till all the water evaporates and the chicken becomes almost dry. This ensures that all the raw flavours of chicken, onions, etc. are removed.

Add now the tomatoes and the yoghurt.

Stir well again and add the salt.

Let the tomatoes cook well.

Now, add a cup of water, and close the lid of the pressure cooker with weight.

Let it come to full pressure (i.e. when the weight lifts and there is a whistling sound).

Turn the heat to low and cook for another 5 minutes.

Remove the weight from the cooker and dry the chicken completely in the open cooker itself.

Method to prepare the chicken using a wok/pan

If not using a pressure cooker, take a wok/pan, add the oil and then put it on your heat source.

As the oil turns hot, add the cumin seeds and let them splutter.

Immediately add the chopped onion.

Stir well till the onions become translucent.

Now, add the chopped ginger and garlic and stir till they start giving off a nice aroma.

Add the chicken and the ghee (clarified butter).

Stir well.

Add the coriander powder, garam masala and the red chilli powder.

Stir and cook the chicken till all the water evaporates and the chicken becomes almost dry. This ensures that all the raw flavours of chicken, onions, etc. are removed.

Add now the tomatoes and the yoghurt.

Stir well again and add the salt.

Let the tomatoes cook well.

Now, add 1-2 cups of water, and cover the wok/pan with a lid.

Turn the heat to low and cook for another 20 minutes or till the chicken is cooked to your liking.

Remove the lid and dry the chicken completely in the wok/pan.

Method for cooking the rice

Separately, in a wok, add the clarified butter along with black cumin seeds, green cardamom, brown cardamom, cinnamon, cloves and bay leaves.

As soon as you start getting a nice aroma, in less than a minute, add the rice along with the salt and sugar.

Do please ensure that the spices brown and not burn, otherwise your dish will be totally spoiled.

Stir well.

Now, add the rice to the cooked chicken in the pressure cooker/wok/pan.

Add the chicken stock, the saffron dissolved in milk and the blanched almonds.

Gently stir so that the mixture is well blended but the rice doesn't break.

If using a pressure cooker

Close the lid of the pressure cooker without the weight and place it on your heat source.

As soon as the steam starts escaping, reduce the heat to low and let it cook for 10 minutes.

Switch off the heat source and let the cooker cool for about 10 minutes before you open it.

This helps all the flavours to seep into the rice and the chicken.

If using a wok/pan

Place the cooked chicken and the prepared rice in a wok/deep thick bottomed vessel along with the chicken stock, saffron and almonds.

Gently stir and then place the vessel on the heat source.

As soon as the stock starts boiling, reduce the heat source and close with a tight fitting lid.

The biryani should be ready in about 15 minutes but you should check by pressing one grain of rice to see if the rice has been properly cooked.

After switching off the heat source, leave the biryani inside the deep pan with the lid tightly shut for another 10 minutes. This helps all the flavours to seep into the rice and the chicken.

That's all. Your delicious chicken biryani is ready.

If using a rice cooker

First of all, wash the rice well (in a vessel 3-4 times, but don't rub it lest the grains break) and let it naturally "dry", on an inclined plate, for 15-20 minutes. This helps enhance the aroma.

Next, prepare the chicken stock. Put in a vessel, the neck and wings of the chicken and pour 4 cups of water over it. Now add ½ inch piece of cinnamon, one green cardamom, and two cloves.

If using pressure cooker, cook under full pressure for 5 minutes.

If not using a pressure cooker, then let the stock be made for half an hour in a wok/deep pan on low heat.

Remove the chicken pieces, strain and keep the stock ready.

Method to prepare the chicken using a pressure cooker

In a pressure cooker, add the oil and then put it on your heat source.

As the oil turns hot, add the cumin seeds and let them splutter.

Immediately add the chopped onion.

Stir well till the onions become translucent.

Now, add the chopped ginger and garlic and stir till they start giving off a nice aroma.

Add the chicken and the ghee (clarified butter).

Stir well.

Add the coriander powder, garam masala and the red chilli powder.

Stir and cook the chicken till all the water evaporates and the chicken becomes almost dry. This ensures that all the raw flavours of chicken, onions, etc. are removed.

Add now the tomatoes and the yoghurt.

Stir well again and add the salt.

Let the tomatoes cook well.

Now, add 1 cup water, and close the lid of the pressure cooker with weight.

Let it come to full pressure (i.e. when the weight lifts and there is a whistling sound).

Turn the heat to low and cook for another 5 minutes.

Remove the weight from the cooker and dry the chicken completely in the open cooker itself.

Method to prepare the chicken using a wok/pan

If not using a pressure cooker, take a wok/pan, add the oil and then put it on your heat source.

As the oil turns hot, add the cumin seeds and let them splutter.

Immediately add the chopped onion.

Stir well till the onions become translucent.

Now, add the chopped ginger and garlic and stir till they start giving off a nice aroma.

Add the chicken and the ghee (clarified butter).

Stir well.

Add the coriander powder, garam masala and the red chilli powder.

Stir and cook the chicken till all the water evaporates and the chicken becomes almost dry. This ensures that all the raw flavours of chicken, onions, etc. are removed.

Add now the tomatoes and the yoghurt.

Stir well again and add the salt.

Let the tomatoes cook well.

Now, add 2 cup water, and cover the wok/pan with a lid.

Turn the heat to low and cook for another 20 minutes or till the chicken is cooked to your liking.

Remove the lid and dry the chicken completely in the wok/pan.

Separately, in a wok, add the clarified butter along with black cumin seeds, green cardamom, brown cardamom, cinnamon, cloves and bay leaves.

As soon as you start getting a nice aroma, in less than a minute, add the rice along with the salt and sugar.

Do please ensure that the spices brown and not burn, otherwise your dish will be totally spoiled.

Stir well.

Now, add the rice to the cooked chicken.

Switch off the heat source and put all the ingredients into the rice cooker.

Add the chicken stock, the saffron dissolved in milk and the blanched almonds.

Gently stir so that the mixture is well blended but the rice doesn't break.

Switch on the rice cooker and let the rice cook. The rice cooker will switch off on its own when the rice is cooked.

Prep time: 30 minutes

Cooking time: 25 minutes with a pressure cooker; 60 minutes with a deep pan; and as indicated in the rice cooker manual

Total time: 55 minutes with a pressure cooker; 90 minutes with a deep pan

Chicken Yakhni Biryani (Chicken Pilaf in a Yoghurt Sauce)

This is a rare biryani which is only cooked on special occasions in Kashmir. Absolutely NIL use of chillies, red or green, makes this dish quite popular with the young and those who just can't tolerate any chillies.

Ingredients

Chicken mince -1/2 Kg (18oz) (2 cups)

Arrowroot powder- 2 tablespoon

Thickly Chopped Onions large-3

Finely Sliced Onions large-2

Chopped Ginger-2 inch

Chopped Garlic-6 cloves

Brown Cardamom (Badi elaichi)-4

Cinnamon (Dalchinni)-3 one inch sticks

Yoghurt unsweetened (Indian set curd is preferred)-1/2 kg (18oz) (2 cups)

Chick pea flour-2 tablespoon

Fennel (Saunf) powder-1/2 teaspoon

Dried Ginger powder-1/2 teaspoon

Bay Leaf (Tej patta)-4

Mint Leaves (Pudina)-15-20 leaves

Clarified Butter (ghee)-2 tablespoon

Long grain rice (Basmati)-2 cups

Salt-1 and ½ teaspoon or to taste

Water- 5 cup

Method

First of all, wash the rice well (in a vessel 3-4 times, but don't rub it lest the grains break) and let it naturally "dry", on an inclined plate, for 15-20 minutes. This helps enhance the aroma.

Now mix the chicken mince with ½ teaspoon salt and the arrowroot powder.

Make walnut-sized balls from this mixture.

In a thick bottomed pan/wok, put the chicken balls, thickly chopped onions, garlic, ginger, brown cardamom, cinnamon and 4 cups of water. Cover with a lid and place it on your heat source.

When the mixture comes to a boil, reduce the heat and cook for 10 minutes or till the chicken balls are cooked.

Leaving the chicken balls in the wok with the water, take out the onion, ginger and garlic pieces and make into a fine paste.

Meanwhile in another wok/pan, beat the yoghurt and chick pea flour well with the fennel powder and dried ginger powder. Add the bay leaves.

Add the onion-ginger-garlic paste and 1 cup water to the yoghurt mixture in the wok.

Now place the wok/pan on your heat source and stir till the mixture becomes almost dry.

Add the chicken balls and the water/stock to this mixture and bring to a boil.

Switch off the heat source.

Now, in another wok/pan, add ghee and put it on your heat source.

When the ghee heats up, add the sliced onion and fry till they are golden brown.

Add the washed and dried rice to this and stir well.

Now add the chicken balls and water/stock to this.

Note: The stock needed to cook the rice should be 4 cups. So in case, this is not so, add more water to make it 4 cups.

Gently stir so that the mixture is well blended but the rice or the chicken balls don't break.

Add the mint leaves.

As soon as the mixture starts boiling, reduce the heat source and close with a tight fitting lid.

The biryani should be ready in about 15 minutes but you should check by pressing one grain of rice to see if the rice has been properly cooked.

After switching off the heat source, leave the biryani inside the deep pan with the lid tightly shut for another 10 minutes. This helps all the flavours to seep into the rice and the chicken.

If using a rice cooker

Place the cooked chicken balls with water and the yoghurt mixture and the prepared rice with fried onions in to the rice cooker.

Stir gently.

Add the mint leaves.

Switch on the rice cooker and let the rice cook. The rice cooker will switch off on its own when the rice is cooked.

Prep time: 15 minutes

Cooking time: 40 minutes with a deep pan; and as indicated in the rice cooker manual

Total time: 55 minutes with a deep pan

Hyderabadi Chicken Biryani

This dish is so phenomenally popular in Hyderabad, in South India, that almost every corner of the city would have an outlet selling it.

The basic difference from the North Indian method is that in Hyderabadi Biryani chicken and rice are cooked separately and then merged.

We present here our "home Style" version which is less greasy and tastier.

Ingredients

Whole chicken -1 approx. 800 grams or 28oz (4 cups) (cut into 8 pieces)

Chopped Onion-3 large

Chopped Ginger-2 inch piece

Chopped Garlic-8 Cloves

Tomatoes-2

Yoghurt unsweetened (Indian set curd is preferred)-1 table spoon

Coriander (Dhania) powder-2 teaspoon

Garam Masala-1 teaspoon

Tip: If you can't get ready-made garam masala mixture from a nearby Indian store, you can make yours by using 1 black cardamom, 3 green cardamoms, 4 cloves, and 1 inch cinnamon-all ground together for this dish.

Red Chilli powder-1/4 teaspoon (enough only to add flavour and not to make it hot)

Cumin seeds (Jeera)-1/2 teaspoon

Cooking Oil-2 tablespoon

Ghee (Clarified butter)-1 tablespoon

Water- 1 cup (just to ensure that the chicken cooks and doesn't burn)

Cooked rice with a little salt and a teaspoon ghee (clarified butter)-3 cups

Saffron-a few strands dissolved in one fourth cup milk

Blanched and fried Almonds-3 tablespoon

(To blanch almonds, immerse them in half a cup of hot water for 30 minutes. Remove the skin thereafter and fry till a light golden colour is achieved.)

Salt- 1 and ½ teaspoon or to taste

Method for cooking the chicken

In a pressure cooker, add the oil and put it on your heat source.

As the oil heats up, add the cumin seeds and let them splutter.

Immediately add the chopped onions.

Stir well till the onions become translucent.

Now, add the chopped ginger and garlic and stir till they start giving off a nice aroma.

Add the chicken and the ghee (clarified butter).

Stir well.

Add the coriander powder, garam masala and the red chilli powder.

Stir and cook the chicken till all the water evaporates and the chicken becomes almost dry. This process ensures that all the raw flavours of chicken, onions, etc. are removed.

Add now the tomatoes and the yoghurt.

Stir well again and add the salt.

Let the tomatoes cook well.

Now, add the water, and close the lid of the pressure cooker with weight.

Let it come to full pressure (i.e. when the weight lifts and there is a whistling sound).

Turn the heat to low and cook for another 5 minutes.

Remove the weight from the cooker and dry the chicken completely in the open cooker itself.

If not using a pressure cooker, then use a wok/pan and cook the chicken thoroughly to your liking.

Method for making the biryani

Layer a deep pan with the rice in one layer and chicken pieces with the gravy in another. Repeat.

Finally cover with rice and pour the saffron and milk over it.

Sprinkle the almonds.

Cover with an aluminium foil and place it in the oven at 150 degrees C (302 degrees F) for 15 minutes.

Prep time: 30 minutes

Cooking time: 40 minutes with a pressure cooker; 75 minutes with a deep pan

Total time: 70 minutes with a pressure cooker; 105 minutes with a deep pan

Chicken Kofta (Mince ball) Biryani

This is another variation from North India that uses chicken mince instead of whole chicken. Can be quite a hit with people who don't want to mess around with chicken bones.

Ingredients

For the chicken Kofta (Mince balls):

Chicken mince -1/2 Kg (18oz) (2 cups)

Onion-2 large (chopped)

Ginger-2 inch piece

Garlic-8 Cloves

Tomatoes-3 (chopped)

(Onion + Ginger + Garlic + Tomatoes blended and made into a fine paste)

Coriander (Dhania) powder-2 teaspoon

Turmeric (Haldi) powder-1 teaspoon

Garam Masala-1+1/2 teaspoon

Tip: If you can't get ready-made garam masala mixture from a nearby Indian store, you can make yours by using 2 black cardamom, 4 green cardamoms, 6 cloves, and 1.5 inch cinnamon-all ground together for this dish.

Red Chilli powder-1/4 teaspoon (enough only to add flavour and not to make it spicy)

Cumin (Jeera) seeds-1/2 teaspoon

Cooking Oil-3 tablespoon

Ghee (Clarified butter)-1 tablespoon

Water-1/2 cup

Bread-2 slices soaked in water

Egg-1

Salt- 1 teaspoon or to taste

For the rice:

Long grain rice (Basmati)-2 cups

Chicken stock-4 cups

Black Cumin seeds (Shahi Jeera)-1/2 teaspoon

Green Cardamom (Chhoti elaichi)-4

Brown Cardamom (Badi elaichi)-2

Cinnamon (Dalchini)-1 inch

Cloves (Laung)-6

Bay leaf (Tejpatta)-1

Clarified butter (Ghee)-1 tablespoon

Salt- ½ teaspoon or to taste

Sugar-1/2 teaspoon

Few strands of saffron dissolved in ¼ cup milk

Blanched Almonds-24 kernels

(To blanch almonds, immerse them in half a cup of hot water for 30 minutes. Remove the skin thereafter.)

Method

First of all, wash the rice well (in a vessel 3-4 times, but don't rub it lest the grains break) and let it naturally "dry", on an inclined plate, for 15-20 minutes. This helps enhance the aroma.

Next, prepare the chicken stock. Take the neck and wings of the chicken and pour 4 cups of water over it along with ½ inch piece of cinnamon, one green cardamom, and two cloves. If using pressure cooker, cook under full pressure for 5 minutes. If not using a pressure cooker then let the stock be made in a wok/pan for half an hour on low heat.

Remove the chicken pieces, strain and keep the stock ready.

Now, prepare the chicken Kofta:

In a bowl, mix together the chicken mince, one egg, half teaspoon garam masala and salt.

Add the bread slices after squeezing out all the water.

Make into walnut size balls.

In a frying pan, add the cooking oil and gently fry these balls 2-3 at a time and keep it in a plate.

Switch off the heat source.

In a pressure cooker/wok/pan, pour the oil from the pan and put it on your heat source.

As the oil turns hot, add the cumin seeds and let it splutter.

Immediately add the Onion + Ginger + Garlic + Tomatoes fine paste.

Stir well till the paste starts giving off a nice aroma and you can see the oil ooze out from the sides.

Add the coriander powder, turmeric, remaining 1 spoon of garam masala and red chilli powder.

Stir well again and add the salt.

Now, add the water.

As the mixture comes to a boil, gently add the fried chicken mince balls.

If using a pressure cooker, close its lid with weight and let it come to full pressure (i.e. when the weight lifts and there is a whistling sound).

Immediately reduce the heat (to SIM on a gas stove) and let the chicken mince balls cook for 2 more minutes before turning off the heat source.

Let the cooker cool down on its own.

In case you wish to use a wok/deep pan, cover that with a tight fitting lid and cook for about 20 minutes or till the Koftas are completely cooked.

Now, add the rice to the cooked chicken Kofta in the pressure cooker/wok/pan.

Add the chicken stock and the saffron dissolved in milk and the blanched almonds.

Gently stir so that the mixture is well blended but the rice or the Koftas don't break.

If using a pressure cooker

Close its lid without the weight and place it on the heat source.

As soon as the steam starts escaping, reduce the heat to low and let it cook for 10 minutes.

Switch off the heat source thereafter and let the cooker cool for about 10 minutes before opening. This helps all the flavours to seep into the rice and the chicken kofta.

That's all. Your delicious chicken Kofta biryani is ready.

In case not using a pressure cooker

Then place the cooked chicken Koftas and the prepared rice in a deep thick bottomed vessel along with the chicken stock, saffron and almonds.

Gently stir and then place the vessel on the heat source.

As soon as the stock starts boiling, reduce the heat source and close with a tight fitting lid.

The biryani should be ready in about 15 minutes but you should check by pressing one grain of rice to see if the rice has been properly cooked.

After switching off the heat source, leave the biryani inside the pressure cooker/deep pan with the lid tightly shut for another 10 minutes. This helps all the flavours to seep into the rice and the chicken.

If using a rice cooker

Place the cooked chicken koftas and the prepared rice in to the rice cooker.

Add the chicken stock, saffron and almonds.

Stir gently.

Switch on the rice cooker and let the rice cook. The rice cooker will switch off on its own when the rice is cooked.

Prep time: 15 minutes

Cooking time: 15 minutes with a pressure cooker; 40 minutes with a deep pan; and as indicated in the rice cooker manual

Total time: 30 minutes with a pressure cooker; 55 minutes with a deep pan

Chicken Stir Fried Rice

Another gem from North-Eastern India. Adding rice makes this a complete dish. You may also find this dish on the menu of quite a few "Chinese" eateries in India.

An excellent way to freshen up your left over rice.

Serves 3-4

Ingredients

Cooked Boiled rice-2 cups

Chicken boiled-boneless-200 grams (7oz) (1 cup)

Chopped Onion-1

Chopped Red Pepper-1

Chopped Garlic-4 cloves

Tomato Puree-2 tablespoon

Soya Sauce-1 + ½ tablespoon

Vinegar-1/2 teaspoon

Red Chilli Sauce-1/2 teaspoon

Sugar-1/2 teaspoon

Salt- ½ teaspoon or to taste

Cooking Oil- 1 tablespoon

Method

In a wok, add 1 tablespoon cooking oil and as soon as it warms up, add the chopped garlic cloves.

As soon as the garlic starts giving off a nice aroma, add the chopped onions and sauté till the onion becomes translucent.

Now add the chicken, soya sauce, red chilli sauce, vinegar, sugar, salt and the tomato puree.

Stir well.

Now add the red peppers and stir till the red peppers are lightly cooked.

Add the boiled rice, and again stir well so that all the ingredients are well mixed.

Switch off the heat source.

That's all. Your Chicken Fried Rice is ready.

Prep time: 10 minutes (excluding the time for boiling the chicken and the rice)

Cooking time: 10 minutes

Total time: 20 minutes

Chapter 7

On the Side

As mentioned, Indians everywhere like to enjoy their curries with simple boiled rice. Occasionally, with dry dishes, or with thicker curries, they may (especially in Punjab) try out rotis (the Indian unleavened bread).

No harm then, if I share the recipes for making simple rice and roti too in this book to turn this into a complete Chicken Cookbook.

Rice Boiled

Ingredients

Rice-1 cup

Water-2 cups

Tip: Use the same cup please! Otherwise, your rice will NOT turn out to be fluffy.

Wash the rice well (in a vessel 3-4 times, but don't rub it lest the grains break) and let it naturally "dry", on an inclined plate, for 15-20 minutes. This helps enhance the aroma.

If you have a Rice Cooker, follow its instructions. Otherwise, I present three popular methods below to turn out a perfect plate of boiled rice.

Method using a pressure cooker

In a pressure cooker (3-5 litre capacity or 6-11 US pints capacity) bring the water to a boil.

Add the rice to the boiling water.

Close the lid of the pressure cooker BUT remove the weight.

When steam starts escaping from the vent (don't worry, you will hear that typical sound), reduce the heat to minimum. In other words, if cooking on gas, turn the knob to SIM (mer).

Wait for 10 minutes and switch off the gas.

Take out the rice. Your hot fluffy rice is ready.

Method using a thick bottomed vessel/deep pan

In a vessel or a pan, bring the water to a boil.

Add the rice to the boiling water. Turn the heat to low and cover the vessel/deep pan with a well-fitting lid.

Cook for 15-20 minutes without stirring the rice. Switch off the heat source. Lift the lid and check whether the rice is properly cooked.

Cooked rice is always soft. To check, you have to take out a grain of rice and press it between your fingers (obviously use a spoon to take out the grain to avoid scalding your hands).

If the grain is still hard, that means it is under cooked. If it is soft, then it is cooked properly.

In case the grain is not properly cooked, you may like to add another ½ cup of water and let it cook on low heat for another 7-10 minutes.

Traditional method (the way it is cooked in villages or dhabas even today)

In a vessel or a pan, bring three (instead of two, mentioned in the above two methods) cups of water (for one cup of rice) to a boil.

Add the rice to the boiling water. Turn the heat to medium and don't cover the vessel/deep pan, because the water will boil and spill over.

Cook for 15-20 minutes stirring the rice gently from time to time. Keep on checking whether the rice is properly cooked.

Once the rice is done, switch off the heat source. Drain all the excess water. You can use a colander. (Traditionally, the vessel will just be covered with a lid and the water poured out. This is tricky as both the vessel and the water would be very hot.)

Although the traditional method takes more time, it is believed to bring out the flavours better. Since the water used for boiling the rice is totally drained out, some dieticians claim that this method helps take out some of the starch from the rice thus shaving off some calories from this dish.

Tip: The drained out water can act as an excellent stock for soups especially when it comes out of the local red coloured rice.

Method using a rice cooker

Place the rice and water in the rice cooker.

Close the lid and switch on the cooker. The rice will be cooked and the rice cooker will switch off on its own.

This is the easiest and the most fool proof way of making rice.

Prep time: 20 minutes

Cooking time: 10 minutes with a pressure cooker; 15-20 minutes with a deep pan; and as indicated in the rice cooker manual

Total time: 30 minutes with a pressure cooker; 35-40 minutes with a deep pan

(Excerpted from my book: The Ultimate Guide to Cooking Rice the Indian Way, which contains 34 more such rice dishes.)

The Classic Indian Roti/Phulka/Chapati

This simple Indian bread, free of yeast or any other leavening agent, is what many Indian homes have every day for lunch or dinner. It is surprising then that most restaurants don't have chapatis on their menus. Instead they focus on making Tandoori Rotis or Nans, which they probably find easier to handle when larger numbers are to be served.

For most households, however, it won't be easy to invest in a Tandoor (earthen oven). For them then it will have to be the simple, non-fussy Chapati. And here's how you can go about making these.

Note: I have seen people rolling dough with a steel tumbler on any flat surface, or using just their hands to give dough the roundish shape of a roti. I think it prudent, however, for all newbies to invest in a rolling pin (belan) and rolling board (chakla) before attempting to make chapatis.

Ingredients

Whole Wheat Flour-3 cups (enough for 5 chapatis)

Luke Warm Water-1 cup

Method

In a mixing bowl, put 2 + ½ cups of flour, reserving ½ cup as parthan (dusting) for rolling out the chapatis later.

Add the water and make into a nice firm dough.

Shape the dough into balls about the size of a large walnut.

In another plate, put the remaining wheat flour (the reserved ½ cup), and press the ball into this dry flour.

At this point, take a thick griddle and put it on your heat source.

While the griddle heats up, take out your rolling board (Chakla).

Using a rolling pin (Belan), shape the dough ball (that is already rolled into the dry flour), into a small circular shape as thin as you can make it.

Now, on the heated griddle place this rolled out chapati.

Let it cook a little on one side and then flip over for the other side to also cook.

Using a tong, remove the chapati from the griddle and place it directly on the flame.

The chapati will immediately swell up and will be ready to be served.

In case you don't have a heat source with a flame, then you will have to puff up the chapati on the griddle itself. For this you will need a handkerchief with which you should gently press the edges of the chapati as it swells on the griddle flipping it for a second time.

Prep time: 5 minutes

Cooking time: 5 minutes for 5 chapatis @1 minute per chapati

Total time: 10 minutes

(Excerpted from my book: Home Style Indian Cooking In A Jiffy, which contains over 100 exotic Indian recipes including for Poori and Paratha, the two most popular Indian unleavened bread dishes.)

Appendix

An Introduction to Some Basic Indian Spices

It is easy to be overwhelmed with the sheer number and variety of fresh herbs and spices that are commonly used in Indian cuisine. I shouldn't, therefore, make this topic even more complicated by giving the scientific or botanical names of such spices, or where they grow, or how these are harvested and processed. There are many excellent books who have done better justice to this topic.

What I shall attempt here is to just list out some twenty of these spices that you should experiment with when you are just starting out with "Home Style" Indian cooking. The ones in bold are essential for any authentic Indian kitchen. The rest are optional.

The discerning reader may notice the omission of Kastoori Methi (a very fragrant variety of Fenugreek) which is very popular for making curries in Indian restaurants. That's precisely the reason why I am leaving this out from my list. But if you prefer your food to taste like dhaba food, do go ahead and stock on Kastoori Methi too. Just remember that this is such a strong herb that it will drown the fragrance of all other spices, howsoever expensive they may be. So for heavens, don't use your saffron with Kastoori Methi ever!

I am also leaving out some expensive spices like nutmeg or star aniseed as they are hardly ever used in your day-to-day cooking.

Here is then my list, in alphabetical order.

Ajwain

Ajwain or Ajowan is pale brown in colour and looks somewhat like caraway or cumin. It has a bitter and pungent taste and its flavour is similar to anise and oregano. This spice smells almost exactly like thyme but is more aromatic and less subtle in taste. Even a small amount of Ajwain tends to dominate the flavour of a dish.

Amchur (Dried green mango powder):

This is used for imparting a strong sour taste.

Asafoetida (Hing):

This is used in small quantities for imparting a strong smell. It is considered very healthy for digestive purposes though some people may find the smell unpleasant and strong. Don't use your saffron with Hing, therefore, ever!

Cardamom (Elaichi):

These come in two varieties: one is small, pale-green and the other is large and brown/black. The pale green variety is used in many Indian dishes including desserts. The brown variety is used for making curries or pulaos, but not in sweetmeats.

Chilli (Kashmiri Red variety):

In our recipes, we have suggested the use of Kashmiri Red Chillies as these impart a nice red colour and are not as hot as are the other red chillies. In case, you like your food to be really hot, then you can use the other red chillies available in the market which are much hotter.

Cinnamon (Dalchini):

This looks like the thin bark of a tree and imparts a lovely flavour both to the sweet and curried dishes. In India, however, it is more used for curries as Indians like Cardamom in their desserts much more than Cinnamon.

Cloves (Laung):

These look like dried flower buds and add a lovely flavour to the food. Cloves are supposed to have antiseptic qualities which help preserve food.

Coconut (Nariyal) powder or milk:

This is used commonly in many South Indian and coastal Indian preparations.

Coriander seeds and fresh green leaves (Dhania and Dhania patta):

The dried seeds of Coriander form an essential part of Indian curries and are used quite extensively. The fresh green leaves are used for making Chutneys (Indian sauce) as well as for sprinkling on curries. Since the fresh leaves have a strong flavour, they should only be used by those who really like the flavour.

Cumin seeds (Jeera):

Cumin is another essential ingredient of Indian cuisine and is generally the first spice to go into the heated cooking oil before other items are added.

Curry leaves (Kare-patta):

These leaves have a lovely flavour and are absolutely essential if you like South Indian cuisine. In India, it grows in abundance and so is easily the cheapest herb to use. Generally used fresh, these can also be dried and used as they retain much of their fragrance even in the dried form.

Fennel (Saunf):

This is used for making some dishes and forms a part of the Pach Phoran which is used in East Indian cuisine.

Fenugreek (Methi):

These are small flat seeds which have a slightly bitter flavour and must be used only in the quantities prescribed. They add quite a piquant flavour to the curries or dry dishes they are added to which are liked by many Indians. Lately, Fenugreek has acquired quite a cult status because of its almost magical effect in reducing the severity of Diabetes.

Garam Masala:

This is a mixture in equal quantities of cinnamon, cloves, cardamom (both pale-green and brown variety) and whole black pepper corns. These can be ground together and kept in air tight containers for future use for up to a week. Some dishes can also be made by putting the whole spices in oil/ clarified butter (Ghee).

All lovers of Indian cooking must learn to use this mixture properly. If you cook Indian dishes only occasionally, you may be tempted to use the commercially available Garam Masala powders. Please remember, however, that to economise on costs, some manufacturers skimp on the more expensive ingredients mentioned above and instead add lots of coriander powder, cumin powder, turmeric powder, red chilli powder, etc. to add volume. They even add Kastoori Methi which just drowns the subtle flavours of other Garam Masalas. So do check before you buy such a ready mix of spices.

Mustard seeds black (Rai):

These are black mustard seeds which look the same as the yellow variety but are supposed to be more pungent than their yellow cousins. This mustard seed is used a lot in South Indian and Western Indian cooking.

Turmeric (Haldi):

This is easily the commonest and the most important ingredient in any Indian curry dish. Though it does not have much of a flavour, it has a dark yellow colour and a lot of therapeutic value.

Yoghurt (Dahi):

Not really a spice or herb, yoghurt is frequently used in many Indian dishes. The variety used in cooking is cultured yoghurt and is always unflavoured. That way it comes closest to the Greek variety of yoghurt.

Please note that if you buy ready-made yoghurt from the supermarket, sometimes it splinters when you heat it. This presents an ungainly sight when you are, for example, cooking chicken with yoghurt.

If you so desire then, you can very easily make yoghurt at home using the following method:

First, to start the whole process, you will need to buy some yoghurt. Subsequently about two tablespoons from the yoghurt you make can suffice to make the next home-made batch of yoghurt.

Ingredients

Milk-1 litre (4 cups)

Plain Unsweetened Yoghurt (as starter)-2 tablespoon

Method

Boil the milk well.

Tip: If you don't boil well, your yoghurt will set but will be a little sticky as factory-made yoghurts generally are.

Let the milk cool down to a level where it feels warm but not hot.

You should be able to use your finger for touching the milk without any fear of scalding it.

Beat the yoghurt well and gently add the warm milk.

Mix well.

Now pour this mixture into a bowl and place it in an insulated casserole.

I use an insulated lunch box which has a small heating element built-in. I need to "switch on" this lunch-box for about 30 minutes in really cold weather (where indoor temperatures be below 15 degree C or 59 degree F)

The basic idea is that the milk should remain warm for at least the next three hours.

After that the yoghurt sets on its own.

It is generally advisable to set the yoghurt at night so that you can have fresh yoghurt in the morning. This also ensures that the vessel is not moved during the entire period that the yoghurt is setting because movement spoils the setting.

Prep Time: 5 minutes

Setting Time: 5 hours (minimum three hours)

A Big Thank You for Reading This Book

Thank you so much for purchasing my book.

I know that you could have picked up other similar books on this subject matter but you took a chance with my book.

So a big THANKS for purchasing this book and reading it all the way to the end.

If you liked this book, I shall be grateful if you could do me a small favour. Please take a moment to leave a review on the site you bought this book from, like Amazon, if you are happy.

If not, please tell me directly. Your feedback is of immense value to me as an Author. Your suggestions will help me in writing the kind of books that you love.

Books by the Author in the 'Cooking In A Jiffy' Series

HOW TO CREATE A COMPLETE MEAL IN A JIFFY

Presenting a Cookbook like No Other Cookbook in the World.

From the popular website www.cookinginajiffy.com and the author of a number of Amazon Bestseller cookbooks comes a cookbook that doesn't focus on recipes.

Instead, it shares the secret of creating a Full Meal in around 30 minutes.

To know more, do please go to:

https://booklaunch.io/prasenjeetkumar@hotmail.com/complete-meal-priced

HOME STYLE INDIAN COOKING IN A JIFFY

(Now available also in Italian and Spanish; coming soon in Japanese)

Amazon #1 Best Seller in Indian and Professional Cooking

With an amazing compilation of over 100 delectable Indian dishes, many of which you can't get in any Indian restaurant for love or for money, this is unlike any other Indian Cook book.

What this book focuses on is what Indians eat every day in their homes. It then in a step-by-step manner makes this mysterious, never disclosed, "Home Style" Indian cooking accessible to anyone with a rudimentary knowledge of cooking and a stomach for adventure.

To know more, do please go to:

https://authormarketing.booklaunch.io/prasenjeetkumar@hotmail.com/home-style-indian-cooking-in-a-jiffy

HOW TO COOK IN A JIFFY EVEN IF YOU HAVE
NEVER BOILED AN EGG BEFORE

(Now available also in Portuguese; coming soon in
German and Turkish)

Never boiled an egg before but want to learn the
magic art of cooking? Then don't leave home without
this Survival Cookbook.

Be it healthy college cooking, or cooking for a single
person or even outdoor cooking---this book helps you
survive all situations by teaching you how to cook
literally in a jiffy.

To know more, do please go to:

https://authormarketing.booklaunch.io/prasenjeetk
umar@hotmail.com/how-to-cook-in-a-jiffy

HEALTHY COOKING IN A JIFFY: THE COMPLETE
NO FAD NO DIET HANDBOOK

(Now available also in Portuguese)

*Amazon #1 in Hot New Releases in Health, Fitness &
Dieting> Special Diets> Healthy*

*Amazon #3 Best Seller in Health, Fitness & Dieting>
Special Diets> Healthy*

If you are sick of dieting, counting calories, or gorging
on supplements, do consider investing in this book of
simply sensible cooking and get on to a journey of
eternal joy and happiness.

To know more, do please go to:

https://authormarketing.booklaunch.io/prasenjeetk
umar@hotmail.com/healthy-cooking-in-a-jiffy

THE ULTIMATE GUIDE TO COOKING LENTILS
THE INDIAN WAY

(Now available also in German)

*Amazon #1 Best Seller in Indian Cooking and Rice &
Grains*

Presenting 58 Tastiest Ways to Cook Lentils as
Soups, Curries, Snacks, Full Meals and hold your
breath, Desserts! As only Indians can.

To know more, do please go to:

https://authormarketing.booklaunch.io/prasenjeetk
umar@hotmail.com/lentils-cookbook

THE ULTIMATE GUIDE TO COOKING RICE THE
INDIAN WAY

Amazon #1 in Hot New Releases in Rice & Grains

From a Bed for Curries, to Pilaf, Biryani, Khichdi,
Idli, Dosa, Savouries and Desserts, No One Cooks
Rice as Lovingly as the Indians Do.

To know more, do please go to:

https://authormarketing.booklaunch.io/prasenjeetk umar@hotmail.com/the-ultimate-guide-to-cooking-rice-the-indian-way

THE ULTIMATE GUIDE TO COOKING FISH THE INDIAN WAY

43 Mouth-watering Ways to Cooking Fish in a JIFFY as Only Indians Can.

So say bye to the boring boiled and broiled ways to make fish and prawn dishes and let this new book open your eyes to the wonderful possibilities of cooking fish the way northern, southern, eastern and western Indians do.

There are six starter (or dry) dishes, 14 curries, 12 prawn dishes, and 4 ways to cook fish head and eggs (caviar) the Indian way.

For the spice-challenged or nostalgia ridden folks, there are 7 dishes from the days of the British Raj.

So if you were wondering how to incorporate fish or this superb, dripping with long strands of polyunsaturated essential omega-3 fatty acids (that the human body can't naturally produce), low-calorie, high quality protein rich white meat in your daily diet, just grab this book with both your hands.

To know more, do please go to:

https://authormarketing.booklaunch.io/prasenjeetk umar@hotmail.com/the-ultimate-guide-to-cooking-fish-the-indian-way

Books by the Author in the 'Quiet Phoenix' Series

CELEBRATING QUIET PEOPLE: UPLIFTING STORIES FOR INTROVERTS AND HIGHLY SENSITIVE PERSONS

(Now available also in Portuguese and Spanish)

Celebrating Quiet People: A unique collection of motivational, inspirational and uplifting TRUE stories for introverts and highly sensitive persons that you shouldn't miss....

From the Amazon #1 best-selling author of the "Quiet Phoenix" series of books comes an outstanding collection of biographies and events that guarantee to increase your self-compassion and self-esteem, regardless of your age, gender or status in society.

To know more, do please go to:

https://booklaunch.io/prasenjeetkumar@hotmail.com/cqp-priced

QUIET PHOENIX: AN INTROVERT'S GUIDE TO RISING IN CAREER & LIFE

(Now available also in Italian; coming soon in Portuguese and Spanish)

Amazon #1 Best Seller in Legal Profession and Ethics & Professional Responsibility

Like the legendary Phoenix bird rising from the ashes, "Quiet Phoenix" is an incredible career change story that Prasenjeet Kumar shares, with wit and charm, of the journey from being a Corporate Lawyer to becoming a Full Time Author-Entrepreneur using his introversion as a strength to overcome all obstacles.

To know more, do please go to:

https://authormarketing.booklaunch.io/prasenjeetkumar@hotmail.com/quietphoenix

QUIET PHOENIX 2: FROM FAILURE TO FULFILMENT: A MEMOIR OF AN INTROVERTED CHILD

(Coming soon in Japanese)

Amazon #1 Hot New Releases in Biographies & Memoirs > Professional and Academics > Educators

Celebrating The Quiet Child: A Must Read For every Parent, Teacher, Mentor, Sports Coach........

Based on the author's own childhood experiences, the underlying theme of the book is that just as a Phoenix Bird is hardwired to be reborn from the ashes of her ancestors, her tears are meant to cure wounds and the way she symbolises undying hope and optimism, so is your Quiet Child built for persistence, creativity, and self-discipline. She will also, without any goading, display a knack for self-learning, high emotional intelligence and an impeccable sense of moral responsibility.

So nurture and celebrate that Quiet Child.

To know more, do please go to:

https://authormarketing.booklaunch.io/prasenjeetk umar@hotmail.com/quietphoenix2-priced

CELEBRATING QUIET LEADERS: UPLIFTING STORIES OF INTROVERTED LEADERS WHO CHANGED HISTORY

What do you think is common between George Washington and the Buddha, Mustafa Kemal Atatürk and Nelson Mandela, Rosa Parks and Florence Nightingale.........

That they were great leaders?

True. But did you know that they were also all introverts?

From Prasenjeet Kumar, the Amazon #1 best-selling author, comes an outstanding collection of uplifting stories of the greatest leaders of all times that have used their powers of introversion to rewrite History.

Most importantly, these leaders succeeded not because they could overcome their introversion, BUT because of their gifted strengths of introversion.

So, ladies and gentlemen, be prepared to immerse yourselves into legendary tales of courage and valour shown by quiet, shy and sensitive men and women from all around the world.

To know more, do please go to:

https://booklaunch.io/prasenjeetkumar@hotmail.com/celebrating-quiet-leaders

Books by the Author in the 'Self-Publishing WITHOUT SPENDING A DIME' Series

HOW TO BE AN AUTHOR ENTREPRENEUR WITHOUT SPENDING A DIME

Are you making the same costly mistakes that Authors usually make?

If so, then here is a book that can help realize your author-entrepreneur dreams WITHOUT SPENDING A DIME.

This book contains everything you need to know about self-publishing and also contains a list of helpful video tutorials and resources.

Here is the link:

https://booklaunch.io/prasenjeetkumar@hotmail.com/author-entrepreneur-priced

HOW TO TRANSLATE YOUR BOOKS WITHOUT SPENDING A DIME

Enca$h the power of translation WITHOUT SPENDING A DIME.

Remember Paulo Coelho's "The Alchemist"? Could it be setting a Guinness World Record if it had not sold more than 65 million copies in 67 different languages?

So if you too could translate your bestseller FROM ENGLISH INTO DIFFERENT WORLD LANGUAGES, it could mean reaching such newer, untapped, unexplored markets whose existence you were blissfully unaware of.

Interested? Then grab this DIY manual of practical tips and advice that can take your writing dreams to literally translation Nirvana.

To know more, do please go to:

https://booklaunch.io/prasenjeetkumar@hotmail.com/how-to-translate-priced

Connect With the Author

As you all know, all the recipes for this book, as well as for all the books in the "Cooking In A Jiffy" series of books are contributed by my mother Sonali Kumar.

This selfless act to share her "Home Style" recipes will, I hope, encourage many other Home Cooks from all over the world to share their family's "secret sauces", thus creating a "Cooking In A Jiffy" revolution that my website www.cookinginajiffy.com has been so valiantly trying to engineer for quite some time.

So to all my readers and well-wishers, who wish to contribute similar "Home Style" recipes from their parts of the world, here's once again a full throated invitation to come join us and make COOKING IN A JIFFY a world-wide movement for home-style cooking that is nutritious and that celebrates family collaboration in cooking above everything else.

The terms are simple. You contribute the recipes, and I edit, format, package and market them. Your name as a writer would come first. You pay nothing upfront but get 50% of all revenues. Deal?

Who then is giving me "Home Style Thai/Korean/Japanese... Cooking In A Jiffy" or "The Ultimate Guide to Cooking Poultry the Chinese/French/Vietnamese/Filipino Way"?

I look forward to hearing from you soon.

Even otherwise, should you have any questions or comments, please do not hesitate to write to me anytime at ciaj@cookinginajiffy.com

I would also love to connect with you on Social Media. Join me on:

Facebook:

https://www.facebook.com/cookinginajiffy

Twitter:

https://twitter.com/CookinginaJiffy

Goodreads:

https://www.goodreads.com/prasenjeet

Google Plus:

https://www.google.com/+PrasenjeetKumarAuthor

About The Author

 Prasenjeet Kumar is the author of over 14 books in three genres: cookbooks (Cooking In A Jiffy series), motivational books for introverts (the Quiet Phoenix series) and books on self-publishing (Self-Publishing Without Spending a Dime series). 8 out of these have also been translated into Spanish, Portuguese, Italian, and German.

Prasenjeet Kumar is a Law graduate from the University College London (2005-2008), London University and a Philosophy Honours graduate from St. Stephen's College (2002-2005), Delhi University. In addition, he holds a Legal Practice Course (LPC) Diploma from College of Law, Bloomsbury, London.

Prasenjeet loves gourmet food, music, films, golf and travelling. He has already covered seventeen countries including Canada, China, Denmark, Dubai, Germany, Hong Kong, Indonesia, Macau, Malaysia, Sharjah, Sweden, Switzerland, Thailand, Turkey, UK, Uzbekistan, and the USA.

Prasenjeet is the self-taught designer, writer, editor and proud owner of the website cookinginajiffy.com which he has dedicated to his mother. He is also running another website publishwithprasen.com where he shares tips about writing and self-publishing.

Index

20847837R00153

Printed in Great Britain
by Amazon